THE MIRACLE OF FATHER KAPAUN

THE MIRACLE
OF FATHER KAPAUN

Priest, Soldier, Korean War Hero

By
Roy Wenzl
and
Travis Heying

IGNATIUS PRESS   SAN FRANCISCO

Cover photos:
Top image: *Fr. Emil Kapaun Celebrating Mass in the Field*
Courtesy of Colonel R. A. Skeehan
Bottom image: *Fr. Kapaun Helping a Wounded GI off a Battlefield*
ACME Photo

Cover design by John Herreid

© 2013 by the *Wichita Eagle*, Wichita, Kansas
All rights reserved
Published 2013 by Ignatius Press, San Francisco
ISBN 978-1-62164-065-3 (PB)
ISBN 978-1-68149-521-7 (eBook)
Library of Congress Control Number 2012942823
Printed in the United States of America ∞

CONTENTS

FOREWORD

Before coming to the Diocese of Wichita as bishop in 2005, I knew nothing about Father Emil Kapaun; I had never even heard his name.

I quickly learned, though, that I was in the minority, not only in the Diocese of Wichita, where Father Kapaun was ordained and served as a priest, but also nationally and even internationally; a lot of people knew a lot about him.

Indeed, there has been interest in Father Kapaun ever since the end of the Korean War, when, after learning of his death in a POW camp, soldiers began telling stories about Chaplain Kapaun. Here is one of my favorites:

Before being sent to Korea, while stationed at Fort Bliss, Texas, Father Kapaun was assigned to bunk with another soldier, a non-Catholic. Not wanting to have a Catholic chaplain as a roommate, the soldier objected and asked for someone else, but his request was denied. Before long Father Kapaun won him over, received him into the Catholic Church, and even witnessed his marriage.

So far the story is only half-told. The soldier and his wife were not able to have children. The doctors said that the wife had an irreversible condition that made conception impossible. After the Korean conflict, the soldier learned that Father Kapaun had died in the POW camp, and he and his wife got the idea of asking Father Kapaun to intercede before the throne of God on their behalf, so that they might have children. Three children later, the doctors still insisted that the woman had an irreversible condition that made conception impossible.

Why all the knowledge of and interest in Father Kapaun? The best answer I can think of is the attraction of his qualities of character.

Father Kapaun was brave. He mocked the Communist indoctrination lectures in the POW camp, calmly refuting their attacks on religion.

Father Kapaun was generous. He literally carried a wounded soldier on a long, torturous forced march to the prison camp.

Father Kapaun was good-natured. He worked at lifting the spirits of the POWs and at giving them hope. "Have faith, have faith", Father Kapaun told them. "Don't give up. We'll get out of here someday."

Father Kapaun was caring. He would wash the clothes and bodies of sick POWs. He would scrounge for extra food to give them, sometimes giving them something from his meager share.

Father Kapaun was self-sacrificing. He was captured because he would not leave the wounded GIs, even though he had the opportunity to do so. He died on May 23, 1951, his death hastened by harsh treatment from his captors and by a lack of food and clothing, for he had given to other POWs much of what he had.

Father Kapaun, just like every human being, including those already canonized by the Catholic Church, was not perfect. For example, he expressed the desire upon being liberated to treat a particularly nasty prison commander to a kick in the bohunkus. But it is his qualities of character, seen together with his humanness, that explain why everyone is interested in and touched by the story of Father Kapaun. These are manly, even heroic qualities of character, and the POWs with him, whether Catholics, Protestants, Jews, Muslims or nonbelievers, found them to be attractive.

There is, however, another layer to Father Kapaun: his motivation, that is, why he acted so bravely, generously, cheerfully, thoughtfully, sacrificially. This can be explained by one word: Jesus.

Jesus gave the gift of himself in love, as shown by his incarnation, ministering as an itinerant preacher, feeding hungry people literally and spiritually, healing their wounds, forgiving their sins and finally losing his life, offering it up and laying it down for others.

Father Kapaun did what he did to imitate Jesus. Like Jesus, Father Kapaun even forgave those who hated him and persecuted him. He told a fellow prisoner who questioned whether they should forgive their brutal guards, "Of course we should forgive them. We should not only forgive our enemies but love them, too. If we fail to forgive, we're rejecting our own faith."

Later, after Father Kapaun's death, the POWs who knew him remarked that the face of Christ on the crucifix carved by a Jewish prisoner—who had never met Father Kapaun, but who daily heard story after story about the priest—looked surprisingly like the face of the heroic chaplain. The prisoner who carved the cross thought that this is what Jesus must have looked like: like Father Kapaun.

With his qualities of character and his Catholic faith, Father Kapaun was, as was said about him by his fellow POWs and is now carved into his memorial in his hometown of Pilsen, Kansas, "all man, all priest".

This is why people ask Father Kapaun to pray for them, to intercede for their intentions. This is why they pray with Bob McGreevy, a survivor of the POW camp who shortly after Father Kapaun's death cried out in his need: "Father Kapaun, help me!"

In fact, before he was taken away to die, Father Kapaun promised the other prisoners: "When I get up [to heaven], I'll say a prayer for all of you." And to one of them, who needed to straighten out his marriage upon his return home, Father Kapaun threatened that if he did not, he would come down from heaven and kick him in the—well, one can guess where.

And this is also why the petition for Father Kapaun's beatification and canonization was made. For if the Catholic Church were to declare him Blessed and Saint, he would inspire yet more people to imitate, as he did, Jesus' gift of self in love, as well as intercede for their petitions before the Divine Majesty.

Whether you know nothing about Father Emil Kapaun or have read other books or articles about him, you will be grateful that you took the time to read this one. I am glad that I did.

+ Michael O. Jackels
Bishop of Wichita
July 2012

INTRODUCTION

Some people regard the meek man as one who will not put up a fight for anything but will let others run over him. . . . In fact from human experience we know that to accomplish anything good a person must make an effort; and making an effort is putting up a fight against the obstacles.

—Father Emil Kapaun

Emil Kapaun is a rare man. The Vatican is considering whether the priest deserves to be canonized a saint, and the president of the United States is pondering whether the soldier is worthy of the Congressional Medal of Honor.

There was nothing remarkable about Emil Kapaun's childhood or early manhood to suggest that he would become a Korean War hero and might someday be declared a Catholic saint. He grew up on a farm in Kansas, where he was born in the kitchen on April 20, 1916. His parents were pious and hardworking, but so were lots of farmers in America's heartland.

Kapaun was a good student at the local public school and later at an abbey high school and college, but with his quiet and unassuming manner he did not stand out as exceptional. His early priesthood and military chaplaincy were uneventful.

When we began the research for Kapaun's story, the chief investigator of his cause for sainthood confided some concerns about his own work. Rev. John Hotze had spent a decade investigating Kapaun for the Vatican. He said one of the frustrating things about talking to Kapaun's Catholic supporters is that many of them used clichés to describe him—surrounding the man's actions with choirs of angels singing and playing harps: "He was such a holy man."

Years ago, some initial Church investigators appeared to seek the same type of descriptions when they questioned Kapaun's fellow prisoners of war. They asked those survivors of North Korea's POW camps whether Kapaun prayed "fervently" every day; whether he was "holy" at all times; and whether dying soldiers got up and walked immediately after Kapaun had laid his hands on them. Although the questions irritated Kapaun's battle-scarred friends, they answered them politely enough.

The Kapaun these friends remembered, however, was no painted-plaster saint. He was a regular guy. He did ordinary things. And he stank and looked dirty because the POWs never got to bathe.

Kapaun saved hundreds of lives, said Lt. Mike Dowe, but not "by levitating himself two feet off the ground". He did practical things, such as boiling water and picking lice—tasks that can seem small but that made a huge difference for malnourished and sick POWs. The mostly soft-spoken man had a temper, Dowe recalled, and he sometimes used colorful language to get his point across.

This gritty reality was just the kind of thing Hotze intended to track down, he explained to us, as clichés would not do the job. Andrea Ambrosi, the Vatican investigator who helped Hotze prepare Kapaun's documents for the Vatican, had told him that Rome wanted the real Kapaun—warts, rags and all.

The job appealed to Hotze, a Wichita Diocese priest who tells good stories in his Sunday homilies. Hotze knew that many great saints down through the ages had been bad boys before their conversions. Paul and Augustine: notorious. Francis of Assisi: as fond of ladies as he was of wining and dining. Although not everyone makes a dramatic 180-degree turn on his way to his best self, every man is in need of conversion; each one has weaknesses and has done things he regrets. Hotze thought the flawed Kapaun would be not only more believable, but more able to offer hope to those who struggle to overcome their failings.

Hotze gathered for the Vatican stories about Kapaun told by non-Catholic POWs—the Protestants, Jews, agnostics and atheists who had no qualms about relating the priest's foibles. And so far, Rome has given Kapaun the title Servant of God, the first of four steps toward canonization.

Hotze's approach shaped the way we wrote our own story for the *Wichita Eagle* in 2009. We too wanted to show Kapaun as he really was.

This book is based on what Kapaun's fellow soldiers told photographer Travis Heying and me about the priest's actions in the Korean War. Although we went in search of the real man, we nevertheless heard stories about Kapaun that sounded miraculous, and for newspaper reporters and editors, the miraculous creates challenges. What soldiers say Kapaun did is so heroic that it defies believability. He saved hundreds of lives, they say, while placing his own at risk. How could such a story be written credibly?

Travis and I began our research by calling Dowe, Herb Miller and Kapaun's other prisoner-of-war friends in June 2009. We drove or flew all over the United States to talk with them. We saw firsthand that they had suffered deeply.

They are still suffering. They choked up sometimes as they told us what they had experienced.

We admired these veterans, but still we wondered whether they had embellished their stories over sixty years of steaks and beers at POW reunion banquets.

One thing that convinced us that Kapaun's friends were telling us the truth was that they demanded *we* tell the truth in what we wrote about him. And we found consistency between what they said and the letters and recorded testimonies that the guys had given about Kapaun over the years.

Kapaun's friends do not consider themselves experts on miracles, but they know what they saw, and as far as they are concerned, the man himself was something like a miracle. By the time we talked to most of them, the secretary of the army and the chairman of the Joint Chiefs of Staff had learned enough about the already decorated U.S. Army captain to recommend him, posthumously, for the highest military honor in the United States. The Pentagon is in the business of declaring war heroes, not saints. But to many of Kapaun's eyewitnesses, they amount to the same thing.

One of the striking things we learned about Kapaun was how little he said on any given day. In civilian life, as in camp, he listened more than he talked. He almost never preached. The chaplain did not even bring up the subject of prayer without permission.

On the march, Kapaun sometimes didn't bother to introduce himself to fellow soldiers as a chaplain or even as an officer. Instead he would throw himself into whatever task they were doing. And then, after the men saw him work harder than any other guy, he would ask whether there was anything more he could do for them, including praying with them.

Some soldiers didn't care for chaplains, considering them Holy Joes who sermonized while grunts did the dirty work. But they liked Kapaun a lot, and one reason was that he made himself one of them. His way of witnessing Jesus was to spare the platitudes and dig foxholes or latrines alongside sweating soldiers.

Another reason the men liked Kapaun was that he treated everyone with respect. He showed Protestants, Jews, Muslims and nonbelievers the same kindness he bestowed on Catholics. Kapaun's friends said this quality stuck out because many people, even many practicing Christians, fail in showing regard to those different from themselves. When Kapaun died, the Muslim Turks in camp revered him as much as anybody else did.

That's who Father Kapaun was. And we know now how he got that way.

In that Kansas farmhouse where he grew up, Kapaun had read the Gospels by kerosene lamplight. In those pages, he had found a hero to imitate—the Jesus who claimed he was divine but who walked among ordinary men, healing them, feeding them, standing up for the weakest among them and dying for them. Jesus won people over more with actions than with words.

In a homily Kapaun prepared for Palm Sunday 1941, while he was still a young parish priest, he wrote that if a crisis ever came, a person who wants to help others should imitate Christ. And that's what Father Kapaun did.

Roy Wenzl

I

THE BATTLE OF UNSAN

*But the peace which God gives is a gift which exists in
suffering, in want, or even in time of war.*

— Father Emil Kapaun, sermon broadcast on
Armed Forces Radio, Tokyo, Japan, 1950

November 1 is All Saints' Day on the Catholic Church
calendar.

On that day in North Korea in 1950, U.S. Army chaplain Father Emil Kapaun celebrated four Masses for soldiers
in the Third Battalion of the Eighth Cavalry Regiment and
went to bed early in his pup tent south of the village of
Unsan. With him in the little tent was his assistant and driver,
Pfc. Patrick J. Schuler, a young guy from Cincinnati.

All around them, as Third Battalion bedded down in a
cornfield, were clues that foretold the disaster about to over-
take them. With the North Koreans on the run, the Eighth
Cavalry's distant commanders, in Seoul and in Japan, all
seemed to think the war was as good as won. Some of the
men had been told to pack their belongings and get ready
for a victory parade in Tokyo. The generals insisted that

the Chinese would not enter the war. The generals were wrong.

Lt. Bob Wood went into the hills on patrol and listened to enemy officers talking to one another on his radio. When he asked a South Korean what the enemy was saying, the Korean said, "Chinese."

Herb Miller, a tough little sergeant who had fought in World War II, had taken a patrol north and come back with a farmer who told Third Battalion intelligence officers that the surrounding mountains hid tens of thousands of Chinese. The intelligence officers scoffed. Miller, disgusted, watched the farmer go home, then stuffed his pockets with grenades.

Early on November 2, All Souls' Day, Miller took out another patrol to the top of a little rise and bedded down in the dark. By then, although he didn't know it, the First and Second Battalions were already being overrun; the Third Battalion was next.

After midnight, he heard a whistle downslope that sounded like a birdcall. Miller punched the GI sleeping next to him. "That's no birdcall!" he said. "We are in for it!"

They got out of there and headed back to the battalion. But then they saw hundreds of figures moving in the dark, and a bugle blew, and then another, accompanied by the ghostly calls of sheep horns blown by Chinese peasant soldiers. Then machine guns sprayed pink tracer bullets, and mortars began thumping. Wild music broke out in the night, war songs from bugles and thousands of throats.

Kapaun and Schuler had scrambled out of their tent long before this; word had come that First and Second Battalions had already folded and were on the road headed for the rear.

GIs fired flares into the night sky and caught their breath: They saw thousands of Chinese soldiers coming at them. A nineteen-year-old corporal named Bob McGreevy, dropping mortar shells down a tube, saw a forward observer come running.

"Get the hell out of here!" he yelled.

Twenty thousand Chinese, who the generals said were not in North Korea, had rushed out of the hills at the three thousand men of the Eighth Cavalry; the First and Second Battalions withdrew south.

Kapaun and Schuler, driving north, loaded a few of the wounded and brought them south. Then they went back for more, but this time they ran into a Chinese roadblock.

"Stay with the jeep and say your prayers", Kapaun told Schuler. "I'll be back."

He ran to find more wounded, but the Chinese attacked. Schuler, frantic, yelled Kapaun's name again and again. In desperation as the Chinese crept closer, he set the empty jeep on fire to destroy it. He never saw Kapaun again.

Most of the First Battalion would escape; some of the Second Battalion, too. But the eight hundred men of Third Battalion covered the withdrawal, and they were overrun.

Miller, running for cover, found GIs in a ditch quivering like puppies. "Get up!" Miller yelled, kicking them. "Get out of here!" They would not move.

All the GIs had to do to kill Chinese was point a rifle in any direction and shoot. Waves of Chinese reached the heart of the Third Battalion; men fought hand to hand. A machine gunner, Tibor Rubin, shot Chinese by the dozens but saw hundreds more keep coming.

GIs saw Kapaun running from foxhole to foxhole, dragging wounded out, saying prayers over the dying, hearing confessions amid gunfire, ripping open shirts to look at wounds. Men screamed at him to escape, but he ignored them. He had repeated chances to escape, as did Dr. Clarence Anderson, but the priest and the doctor repeatedly ran into the gunfire to drag men into the relative safety of the American perimeter.

Kapaun called McGreevy and others into a huddle.

"I'm going to give you guys the last rites," he said, "because a lot of you guys are not going to make it home."

McGreevy noticed how calm Kapaun looked. The priest called out the sacred words in English, not Latin; the GIs were from all shades of belief.

On the Chinese came. GIs fired bazookas into their own trucks in their own camp and machine-gunned Chinese by the light of the fires. Warplanes dropped napalm, incinerating hundreds of Chinese.

For days, the Third Battalion fought off mass charges of Chinese. They ransacked bodies for weapons and bullets when they ran low.

By that time Kapaun and Anderson had set up an aid station in a sandbagged dugout.

The GI perimeter shrank. Several soldiers who had escaped said their last view of Kapaun came when the American perimeter had shrunk to only about fifty yards across; the men in there were surrounded on all sides by thousands of Chinese. Kapaun was in the middle of it, unhit as of yet, and running from foxhole to foxhole to treat the wounded. He refused to stay in there, though: Lt. Walt Mayo saw Kapaun run three hundred yards outside the lines to drag stray wounded inside.

During one of those runs, Kapaun was captured and led away at gunpoint. But GIs rose up and fired at Kapaun's captors, allowing him to escape.

McGreevy heard officers yell at Kapaun to leave the battlefield.

"No", Kapaun called back.

The officers yelled again.

"No," Kapaun said, "my place is with the wounded."

The priest looked as calm as he did at Mass.

By this time, Kapaun and Anderson had about forty wounded in the dugout, which lay exposed far outside the GI perimeter. The Chinese were digging trenches while advancing, protecting themselves as they moved in. McGreevy could see dirt flying out of the Chinese trenches.

Lt. William "Moose" McClain watched this and thought of Custer's Last Stand.

The sergeant who had heard that first birdcall now lay in a ditch not far from Kapaun's aid station. Miller's ankle had been shattered by a grenade. He had spent hours playing dead.

Once in a while, when a group of Chinese got close, he tossed a grenade, then played dead again. When he ran out of grenades, a nearby wounded GI threw him a few more and Miller tossed them at the Chinese.

The Chinese were all around him now, shooting at the shrinking perimeter. Miller pulled a dead enemy body on top of himself. Soon an enemy soldier sat down in the ditch, his boot touching Miller's arm.

By then, the Chinese had crept near the dugout where Kapaun and Anderson tended the wounded; they fired mortar rounds in there, killing some of the wounded.

Surrender seemed like suicide. The GIs had heard stories of atrocities in Korea. Kapaun had written a friend weeks before that "the Reds were not taking prisoners. So we resolved to fight them to the finish because we would not have a chance if we chose to surrender."

But in the dugout now, Kapaun made a bold move: He approached a captured and wounded Chinese officer. He said he would surrender and appeal to Chinese humanity.

That officer yelled outside. The Chinese stopped shooting at the dugout. They took Kapaun and fifteen or so of the wounded who could walk as prisoners. They also agreed not to shoot the rest of the wounded.

Anderson thought Kapaun's negotiations saved forty lives in the dugout.

Kapaun, under guard, stepped out of the dugout, over dead men piled three high. Down by the road, he saw an enemy rifleman take aim at a GI lying in a ditch.

That rifleman had found Miller hiding under a dead body. He put his rifle muzzle to Miller's head; Miller thought the muzzle looked big enough to crawl into. He would die now. Then he heard footsteps. So did the soldier about to kill him. The soldier, distracted, looked toward the dugout, his rifle still touching Miller's forehead. Miller turned to look.

They saw an American officer walking toward them. He was tall, skinny and unarmed, and he walked as calmly as a man about to pay his grocery bill. Kapaun had walked away from his captors, in the middle of a battle, risking a bullet in the back. But his captors held their fire.

Kapaun walked to the rifleman and shoved him aside, brushing the rifle barrel away from Miller's head with his arm.

"Let me help you up", he said. His voice was calm. He got Miller up on one foot; then helped him onto his back.

Miller turned around to look. The soldier who had wanted to shoot him aimed his rifle but did not fire. He looked puzzled. With Miller on his back, Kapaun walked toward the Chinese who had taken him prisoner at the dugout.

Miller waited for death. But his would-be executioner just let him go.

"He didn't know what to do", Miller said. "Father Kapaun had that effect on those guys."

Miller, with his arms around Kapaun's skinny shoulders, wondered how far the priest could carry him.

2

DEATH MARCH

Men find it easy to follow one who has endeared himself to them.

—Father Emil Kapaun

Survivors at Unsan broke out and fought south through the hills. Schuler, Kapaun's young assistant, dodged Chinese infantry patrols while trying to find the American lines. He plunged into the icy water of what he thought were seven separate rivers during his desperate flight. He later realized, he said with a rueful grin, that he had actually swum across seven bends of the same river. Within days he became the first soldier to give an eyewitness account of Kapaun's heroism to war correspondents desperate for a hero as they wrote about the terrible disaster. The stories went worldwide.

Schuler got away; most men didn't. They were killed or rounded up by Chinese patrols that treated them roughly. Chinese soldiers stole their watches, rings, helmets and boots. Some of the captives thought this was the end, that they would be gunned down. The enemy in Korea frequently tortured and killed prisoners immediately after capture.

Miller, however, his ankle shredded and bleeding, rode away from slaughter on Kapaun's back.

Lt. Walt Mayo, who had saved Kapaun the first time he was captured at Unsan, escaped from the perimeter with his friend Phil Peterson and a dozen others, running across a road covered with dead Chinese. They hid out in a haystack for a while; in three days, they managed to hike eighteen miles south toward the American lines before they ran into a Chinese patrol. Mayo, who had spent four months in a German prisoner-of-war camp in World War II, would now spend thirty-four months in a camp more deadly.

McGreevy, who had watched Kapaun bless men with the last rites, briefly escaped over a carpet of hundreds of dead Chinese in a streambed, their limbs burned and twisted from napalm.

Lt. Ralph Nardella, a tough-talking Italian from New Jersey, was captured before he got out of the perimeter. In six months, Nardella would risk his life to save Kapaun.

———————

Kapaun carried Miller north, under guard with other prisoners. The Chinese let the priest keep his ciborium, the three-inch-wide gold container for Communion hosts.

Miller got a good look at Kapaun: wide-set gray eyes, a sharp nose, a deeply cleft chin and thinning sandy hair; tall in stature and a little short of 175 pounds. The priest said he was from Kansas; Miller told him he was a farm kid from western New York.

The guards yelled at them if they talked, so they couldn't say much more. The Chinese herded them along, mostly without food, mostly at night, in an arduous trek in the cold that survivors later called the Death March. At least,

Kapaun told Miller, if they kept walking like this, they would stay a little warmer.

Korean winters can be bitterly cold, especially in the mountains; this would prove fatal to many. Along the way, shivering men who had not eaten in days began to refuse to carry wounded comrades, a move that meant death for the wounded.

Joe Ramirez, a corporal whom Kapaun had baptized literally on the invasion beach when the Eighth Cavalry landed in Korea in July, was carrying wounded even though he had been hit five times himself.

He saw Kapaun begin to move up and down the line, "practically begging men to carry the wounded." Some did; others hid from officers. Men in the army are expected to follow orders at all times, but that's not how it works in a death march; soldiers on the verge of collapse will follow a sergeant they respect into hell and tell a general to go there.

Kapaun, sensing this, began to carry stretchers without ever taking a break, hoping men would follow his example.

Other streams of prisoners would join theirs; some of them, including Kapaun, would ride occasionally in captured trucks. But for part of the way, Miller rode on the priest's back, amazed that they were both still alive.

"You should put me down", Miller said. "You can't keep this up."

"We'll keep going," Kapaun replied.

Sometimes Miller heard shots from the back of the column, and he understood that the Chinese were shooting those who could not keep up.

On November 4, while the Eighth Cavalry was being overrun to the northeast, Lt. William Funchess of the

Nineteenth Infantry had one of those frustrating conversations that happened a lot at that time in Korea.

Funchess was staring from a hilltop at hundreds of soldiers stripping naked on the bank of the freezing Ch'ongch'on River. They carried clothes and rifles above their heads as they waded across. They marched four abreast in the direction of the battalion headquarters of Funchess' commanders.

Funchess had radioed a commander at headquarters to say the soldiers he saw were not dressed like North Koreans. "They are Chinese", he explained.

"You are mistaken", the commander said. "There are no Chinese in North Korea."

Not long afterward, Funchess heard gunfire coming from headquarters. A short time later, Funchess and Lt. Mike Dowe and the two platoons they commanded were fighting hundreds of Chinese.

In only a few weeks, they would become two of Kapaun's closest friends; they would try to save his life. But first they had to save each other. Dowe and Funchess retreated at last, leading a dozen survivors; they saw soldiers in the distance. Dowe and Funchess told everybody to be quiet, but a GI cupped his hands around his mouth.

"Don't shoot! We're GIs!"

But the soldiers were Chinese, and they sent bullets spattering against the rocks, knocking men down, tearing a hole through Funchess' right foot.

"You're not going to leave me here, Mike?" Funchess asked.

"No", Dowe said.

They tried to run up a small mountainside, with Dowe dragging and carrying Funchess along. They came face-to-face with a Chinese soldier firing a submachine gun, shredding scrub pine needles all around them. They shot back and kept going.

Out of ammunition, they made their way to a ravine, where they looked up at dozens of Chinese aiming rifles at them, a vision Funchess would see for decades in nightmares. They were captured. The Chinese, herding them along, came across half a dozen wounded GIs. When they saw the GIs were too badly injured to stand up, the Chinese rolled them over and shot them in the back of the head, one at a time, as Funchess watched.

They tied up the captured soldiers, binding Dowe with a loop around his neck that choked him if he moved. Dowe watched a Chinese soldier try to remove a ring from the finger of a wounded GI. When the ring stuck, the Chinese cut the finger off with a knife.

Another soldier put a pistol to Dowe's head and pulled the trigger. The pistol was empty; the Chinese soldier laughed.

Hours later, they crowded the Americans into a schoolhouse to rest. In the building were wounded from the Eighth Cavalry. They told Dowe about a heroic Eighth Cavalry chaplain who had saved many lives.

———— // ————

Riding on Kapaun's back, Miller felt guilty. He had never attended the priest's Masses in camp or on the battlefield, although he knew the guy was well liked. Miller had never met him until the priest stopped his execution.

Sometimes other people carried Miller; then the priest carried others, or urged men to carry stretchers, which they made from tree branches and rice sacks scrounged from nearby farms. The branches would dig into the carriers' shoulders. Sometimes, when the carriers would set the stretcher down to change positions, the Chinese would yell to move along, and the wounded soldier was left to die.

Kapaun one night rode in a captured American truck, buried under wounded GIs. He didn't move for fear he would hurt the wounded atop him. When the truck stopped and Kapaun got out, he collapsed, his legs stiff with cold. When he checked his feet he saw frostbite. He limped after that.

But when he found men refusing to pick up the wounded, he picked up stretcher poles himself. Men who had refused to do this for their officers did it when he asked.

At the schoolhouse where Funchess and Dowe spent their first night as prisoners, Funchess shoved his compass and his pocket-size copy of the New Testament into the sock of his undamaged left foot.

Dowe heard prisoners from the Eighth Cavalry say that the reason so many of them were alive was that they had been saved by a doctor named Anderson and a recklessly brave chaplain. Dowe heard the Eighth Cavalry men say the priest's name: "KuhPAWN, Father KuhPAWN."

Funchess, Dowe and other prisoners from the Nineteenth Infantry joined the long line of POWs that included Kapaun, Miller and the Eighth Cavalry. Other groups of prisoners joined theirs; they were given little or no food and ate snow for water.

Funchess stumbled forward, the bones of his right foot mangled. For a while he was carried in one of the rice-bag stretchers. After soldiers had dropped him several times, he walked.

During the days that followed, Chinese soldiers noticed Funchess limping and stumbling. They motioned for him

to sit down. Funchess thought they wanted to shoot him,
so he pretended not to understand.

Kapaun kept moving up and down the line, limping, carrying stretchers, comforting men. Sometimes he would carry
Miller piggyback. When he got tired, he would let Miller
slide down his back, and Miller would hop on one foot
with one of the priest's arms around him. Miller did not
want to wear out the priest, but hopping made his ankle
bleed badly, so Kapaun or somebody else would carry him
some more.

Miller had parachuted into Normandy on D-Day six years
before; he had fought many battles, but he had never seen
anybody like this priest. When carried by Kapaun, Miller
could feel the man's skinny back. There did not appear to
be a lot of muscle there, but the guy seemed to be made of
iron. He kept going hour after hour, living on nothing but
the little ball of millet they got once a day from the guards.

"Father," Miller said, "you need to put me down."

Kapaun shook his head.

"If I put you down, Herb, they will shoot you."

3

PRISONER OF WAR CAMP

Christ's works testified to what he was; our works will testify to what we are.

—Father Emil Kapaun

Several hard days after capture, after more than sixty miles of marching, the starving survivors of the Eighth Cavalry and Nineteenth Infantry straggled into a mud-hut village called Pyoktong, on the banks of the Yalu River, two miles from Manchuria.

They had barely set foot in the village when American bombers roared in overhead and firebombed it. Horrified villagers spat at the prisoners and threw rocks.

Guards took them south again, twelve more miles. Men and discipline broke down in the snow and ice; men left their wounded to die in ditches, ignoring orders from officers to pick them up. They would not ignore Kapaun, though. He walked the line, asking men to help. Many did.

Dowe picked up a stretcher on this march one night, turned around and spoke to the tall soldier carrying the pole behind him.

"Who are you?" he asked.

The soldier reached out a hand. "KuhPAWN", he said.

Dowe grinned. This was the heroic chaplain that Eighth Cavalry prisoners told stories about.

"Father Kapaun! I've heard all about you!"

"Well," Kapaun said in a self-deprecating tone, "don't tell my bishop."

———#———

The mountain valley was three miles long and included the hamlet of Sombakol. Temperatures dropped far below zero; hunger fostered feelings of desperation that worsened every day. The soldiers still had some fight in them; some, Moose McClain included, sneaked into neighboring fields and arranged cornstalks in piles, spelling P-O-W, hoping the U.S. Air Force would take notice.

Guards fed them birdseed twice a day. The two little handfuls of millet and cracked corn provided maybe 300 daily calories at most.

The millet made men gag; they had no hot water to soften it, so the grain did not digest and scratched their intestines like fine sand. Some could not get it all down, but Kapaun begged them to eat everything no matter what.

Tadashi Kaneko, a first sergeant from the Eighth Cavalry's regimental headquarters group, noticed that some of the young soldiers were giving themselves what amounted to a death sentence; soldiers only seventeen or eighteen years old were refusing to eat the grain.

"I can't eat this stuff."

Kapaun and the older soldiers insisted that they must.

Hunger and cold made men cruel; they stole from each other. McClain yelled at the enlisted men for this; Kapaun pleaded with them. McClain sometimes saw Kapaun chide the officers, however, scolding them if they slacked off when it came to helping others.

Men noticed, to their delight, that Kapaun sometimes swore at the guards when he was angry, although he never took the Lord's name in vain.

Sometimes, to calm new young prisoners, Kapaun cracked jokes. "Welcome to our paradise", he would say. Survivors later told author William Maher that when newly captured young soldiers asked Kapaun what the enemy would do with them, the priest gave them a line right out of a GI foxhole: "They're going to shoot the officers and let the enlisted men go."

The priest used more than humor to give encouragement. Ramirez, the corporal Kapaun had baptized on the beach, and Sid Esensten, a doctor, saw him visiting the sick all over the camp, sneaking into huts to avoid the guards, wearing only a light field jacket against intense winter cold.

"Have faith, have faith", Kapaun told Ramirez and the others. "Don't give up. We'll get out of here someday."

Al Brooks, another enlisted man, was in one of these groups. Kapaun told them to hang on to hope. "God is on your side", he said.

Sometimes during these visits the priest would pass around his pipe, to Edmund Reel or other soldiers; it held the last of Kapaun's Prince Albert tobacco.

"You guys wanting a little puff of this, you might as well have it now because what I've got isn't going to last much longer."

In late November a few survivors from Unsan were released. Sgt. Samuel Cleckner made his way to American lines, telling army officers and news reporters that he had seen a chaplain in the enemy camps visiting as many as two hundred soldiers a day, treating wounds, saying the Rosary.

He told them he had promised Kapaun that he would write to Kapaun's parents in Kansas.

Cleckner was the first eyewitness to relate stories of Kapaun's heroism in the camps. Newspapers passed along what he said, along with how Cleckner and others described Kapaun staying behind at Unsan when he could have escaped; how at the end, when the last defenders were overrun, he was the only American officer still on his feet. Cleckner told how Kapaun had refused at first to surrender the dugout with the wounded, thinking the enemy would execute them. He surrendered, Cleckner said, only after the enemy had lobbed grenades and mortar shells into his position and it was clear there was no other choice.

When Cleckner last saw Kapaun, he said, the chaplain seemed to be in good shape, except for one thing—he had lost a lot of weight.

———

The army telegram telling Kapaun's parents that he was missing arrived in Pilsen, Kansas, on Thanksgiving Day 1950. The postman knew that Enos and Bessie Kapaun usually went to noon Mass on Thanksgiving, so he stopped at the Catholic church and handed the telegram to a woman there, asking her to give it to Kapaun's parents. Although the telegram was sealed, the woman thought it might relate bad news; so she went to the rectory next door, distraught at her assignment. The parish priest, Rev. Joseph Goracy, told her he would handle the task.

Goracy years later wrote about his meeting with the Kapauns:

> I asked the couple into the rectory, and after inviting them
> to sit down in the large reception room I calmly told them

of the telegram. Mr. Enos Kapaun, already seventy, was a tall man, rather on the slender side. His shoulders were a little stooped as he sat nervously looking around the room. Mrs. Kapaun, fifty-five years of age, was for once without her perpetual smile. She asked me to open the telegram and read it to them.

Goracy did so. The telegram was from Edward F. Withell, adjutant general of the U.S. Army, who wrote:

> The Secretary of the Army has asked me to express his deep regret that your son Captain Emil J. Kapaun has been missing in action in Korea since Nov. 2nd '50. Upon receipt of further information in this office you will be advised immediately. Confirming letter follows.

Here is how Goracy described the way the Kapauns received the message:

> It was with quiet resignation that these fine parents accepted the news that their son was missing in action. There were a few tears, but they were quiet tears. I did my best to instill some hope into them, which Mrs. Kapaun was quite willing to accept. Mr. Kapaun had only one statement: "I will not see my son again on this earth. I have to wait until I get to heaven."

Kapaun had given Cleckner his parents' address. Cleckner had promptly lost it. He tracked it down later from the army's chaplain service, but that took time; so it was October 1951, nearly a year after his return to American lines in Korea, that Cleckner wrote a letter to Enos and Bessie Kapaun.

By that time, the son he described to the parents was dead; but no one outside of Pyoktong in North Korea knew that yet. Cleckner's handwriting was beautiful and easy to read, and what he told Kapaun's parents, nearly a year after his capture, brought not only a tingle of hope but the first thrilling account of the heroic deeds of faith and courage performed by their soft-spoken and genial son.

6 Oct 1951

We were taken prisoner by the Chinese Communist Army on about the same day. Father Kapaun was taken the day before I was and then later we were together in a prison camp in the interior of North Korea. We shared the same room and my sleeping space was right next to Father Kapaun. When I was released last year to return to our Army I promised to write to you.

May I say that your son is one of the bravest men I have ever met. He showed great courage and devotion to his country and faith under the most hazardous of conditions. I have seen him stand unflinchingly in the face of fire in order to bring comfort and aid to some soldiers that had been wounded or to deliver last rites in some instances. He kept up the morale of those that had been taken prisoner by his kindness and words of hope and faith.

I sincerely wish that the Chinese would have released your son at the same time I was, and hope that you receive even more glad and important news than I can give you.

Sincerely yours,
Samuel J. Cleckner

In the camp, Kapaun continued to show the courage that Cleckner had witnessed. When the POWs began to steal food from the enemy, the man leading the raids was often the chaplain from Kansas.

Kapaun explained to the men that the commandment against stealing did not apply to them because they were being starved to death by their captors.

"Steal or starve," he said, "it's obvious."

Kapaun led the men out into the countryside at night, sneaking past guards. They came back with bits of wood, ears of corn, red peppers torn from frozen bushes, an old pumpkin. Sometimes they even stole bags of grain from a camp warehouse.

Before these sorties, Kapaun lined up the men and asked them to pray for help from Dismas, patron saint of thieves, the Good Thief who was crucified beside Christ. Kapaun said that Saint Dismas would intercede with God for their success.

Mayo and others, doubtful but amused, nicknamed Kapaun, Dismas. He had surprised them for months with his bravery, and now with his ingenious thieving. A notorious thief, Esensten said of him, incredibly devious.

Kapaun would prowl fields and find potatoes or corn the farmers had hidden under shocks of grain. Or he would conspire with Mayo, who was proving to be as resourceful as Kapaun.

Mayo was as handsome as a movie star and highly intelligent, a graduate of Boston University. He was a devout Catholic and a World War II combat veteran who had already survived four months as a prisoner of war in Germany. He admired Kapaun's daring, and when he matched it with his own, the two of them became a fierce pair of conspirators.

Mayo would start an argument with guards at the crib where food was stored, while Kapaun and others, such as Dowe, would sneak inside, stuff their pockets with soybeans or salt, then heave a grain sack across a shoulder and sneak out.

Kapaun ranged widely at Sombakol, giving aid and comfort to everyone he met. One of the POWs who saw this was Lawrence Donovan, a captured medic with C Company of the Sixty-Fifth Regiment of combat engineers in the Twenty-Fifth Infantry Division.

Donovan had seen a lot of combat, from July until November 27, when his outfit was overrun. He was a devout Catholic and said so to the guards. One of them beat him for that and asked: "Where is your God now?"

"He is right here, in my mind and in my heart", Donovan replied. The guard beat him some more.

Donovan saw Kapaun go constantly from group to group, telling men not to give up, telling them they would be liberated. The men believed him, Donovan said, "because we had so little to live on that we lived on false hopes and rumors".

Sometimes, when the POWs heard an explosion in the distance, Kapaun would call out, "That's Allied troops, getting closer. We're getting out of here."

Donovan knew that this was not true; the explosions were set off by Chinese soldiers dropping dynamite in the river and collecting the stunned fish that came up. Kapaun might have known it too, but that didn't stop him from seizing the opportunity to encourage the prisoners with the hope that they would soon go free.

One day, early in their captivity at Sombakol, Donovan and Kapaun found themselves in the same hut; the Koreans finally brought a tub of food to the starving men. The officers and enlisted men crowded around, each preparing to dip a little wooden paddle for his one dollop.

Kapaun spoke up suddenly, and Donovan could hardly believe the priest's audacity in reminding his fellow officers of an old army rule.

"Hey," Kapaun said to his fellow officers, "enlisted men eat first, and officers eat last. Don't you think we ought to let the enlisted men eat first?"

The officers stared at him; then made way for the enlisted men.

Sombakol was the name of the village, but not long after they got there the prisoners called it Kapaun Valley, or more sarcastically, Happy Valley. Whatever the name, Pentagon analysts decades later said the camp at Sombakol had far fewer deaths than others during that period of the war. Esensten said Kapaun was the main reason.

On Christmas Eve 1950, Dowe, McClain, Nardella and two other POWs escaped from Sombakol and hiked south. They knew it might take weeks to find American lines, but they were starving.

After trekking twenty-five miles, McClain wrote later, they "were worn out, wet and sweating" as they sat down to rest. Soon they were freezing. They took a Korean family prisoner in their home, where they ate and slept with one escapee on guard.

They let a little girl in the family go outside to use the toilet, and she ran off. At midnight the girl returned with North Korean soldiers. Hundreds of bullets splintered the walls of the house.

Nardella, who was on guard, shouted, "Men, this is it!" Then he stepped accidentally on the family's hibachi in bare feet. He ran out the door in terrible pain, puzzling the North Koreans as they reloaded. Nardella got them to stop firing, and the Americans found themselves prisoners again.

They were taken to a police station, stripped naked and shoved into cells with dead bodies. They were told they faced execution. Dowe boldly demanded an audience with the police chief. He told the chief that if he spared their lives he would give him something no one else in North Korea had. The chief agreed, and Dowe handed over his West Point class ring. The chief not only spared their lives, but, to their astonishment, took all five to a restaurant on Christmas Day and fed them the first real meal they had eaten since early November. The next day, they were returned to Sombakol, where they resumed starving.

———*———

In January 1951, guards marched prisoners back to Pyoktong. The village turned POW camp was virtually escape-proof. Deep inside North Korea, it was surrounded on three sides by inlets of the dammed-up Yalu River. Before the war Pyoktong had one thousand inhabitants, now it held hundreds of POWs.

The march there was carried out in brutal cold, and Esensten knew ahead of time that some would not survive. Many more men than on the previous march would refuse to carry stretchers.

The doctor had spent weeks watching Kapaun become the most popular man in the camps, the only man the POWs seemed eager to please, a man they respected deeply. Esensten asked Kapaun to use his influence with the men so they would help each other on the march.

Kapaun walked the line, calling out for help, giving encouragement. Nine men died, but Kapaun saved at least four times that number, the doctor thought.

Esensten noticed that Kapaun himself was suffering badly— limping, his sharp nose sticking out between bony cheekbones, a reddish beard covering the rest of his wizened face.

But as weak as he was, the Chinese had begun to fear Father Kapaun. There seemed to be no limit to the man's endurance, and his fellow prisoners turned to him for advice and leadership.

The guards began to heckle Kapaun. What incensed them most was that he defied their ban on religion. Every night the priest sneaked into various huts, where he passed around a little food, his lit pipe and a bit of hope. "Would anyone care to say a little prayer?"

Some atheists said the Rosary with him now.

In Pyoktong, in the winter of 1951, when temperatures reached twenty and thirty and even forty degrees below zero, men began to die every day from starvation, pneumonia and giving up. It was easier to do that than to live.

It was bad enough in January; by February Pyoktong had become a death camp. One day Ramirez counted forty-five bodies in the enlisted men's camp, and he wondered whether he would be next.

The freezing, starving men did desperate things.

When some of them found POW excrement on the ground and noticed soybean seeds that had passed through someone's body without being digested, they picked up the seeds and ate them.

One day a dog wandered among the Americans' huts and let out a bark; Ramirez and others turned him into soup.

According to the Pentagon, of the 3,000 to 4,000 POWs in Pyoktong and surrounding places, 1,300 died that winter. The men were being ravaged by advanced starvation, Esensten explained, which made them prone to disease. They suffered from scabies, scurvy, beriberi, pellagra and dysentery. Esensten counted at least 350 cases of pneumonia every day. Bodies piled up outside huts, frozen stiff in death.

To many men it looked hopeless. But every morning they could count on seeing Kapaun doing something useful. Sometimes they would awaken at 5:00 A.M. to a banging sound and find the bearded priest in his filthy uniform hammering out metal with a stone in his fist. Kapaun had scrounged scraps of tin from bombed-out huts in Pyoktong and was fashioning them into pans for boiling water. He made the pans so expertly that they barely leaked.

Early in the morning Kapaun would collect wood, start a fire and place upon it one of his homemade pans filled with some snow. When the water boiled he would throw in some parched beans or sorghum. "Hot coffee!" he would call out.

Boiling water to purify it probably saved many lives; dysentery alone killed hundreds in the camp. POW Joseph O'Connor said Kapaun also used the boiled water to wash the bodies and the soiled underwear of the wounded and the sick.

Kapaun accidentally injured himself that winter. He chipped a sliver into his eye while chopping wood; the eye got infected. When Warrant Officer Felix McCool inquired for a priest one day, men pointed to a ragged man wearing a black eye patch.

———✦———

Esensten by now had discovered that he felt a strange peace when talking with Kapaun.

They lived in filth and spent much of each day picking lice out of their clothes. They smelled like excrement; no one had bathed in months. The Jewish doctor would forget all this in long talks with Kapaun about philosophy and religion. Esensten knew nothing about Catholicism, but Kapaun knew Judaism thoroughly.

Because Kapaun was the quiet sort of man who does not draw attention to himself, many people who knew him before the war were surprised to learn, long after his death, how smart he was. In the seminary, he had learned shorthand to take down lectures verbatim. He knew Latin

and German, wrote fluently in Czech and had been learning Japanese just before leaving Japan for the landing in
Korea.

Esensten teased Kapaun, though; he thought the priest
was blindly rigid about Church teachings. This puzzled Esensten, who saw how open-minded Kapaun was about everything else. So Esensten argued: Shouldn't morals and other
religious teachings be more flexible in some circumstances,
such as when a man is in a prison camp?

"No", Kapaun said.

But when guards coerced some starving prisoners to
inform on their fellow Americans and some others wanted
to punish the informers, Kapaun defended the guilty, protecting them from harm. The priest did not bend the rules,
Esensten observed, but he was the first to extend forgiveness to a sinner needing mercy.

Funchess met Kapaun for the first time that winter as the
young lieutenant hobbled around the enlisted men's compound on his wounded foot.

Funchess had falsely told guards he was an enlisted man
because he worried they might shoot the American officers. In addition to being in pain, he was hounded by fear;
men died of infections from lesser wounds than his. Like
everybody, he ate snow that he scraped off the ground; there
was no water.

He saw a man bent down, acting strangely. His cap was
a sleeve torn from a GI sweater; he wore an eye patch; he
looked like a hobo, filthy and thin.

The man motioned to Funchess.

Funchess hesitated.

The man beckoned. Funchess hobbled over.

The man was tending a tiny fire. Funchess marveled; the guards at that time had forbidden fires. There was a pot made of rusted tin; it steamed.

"Would you like a drink of hot water?" the man asked.

"Yes! I would!" Funchess said. In his Carolina accent, "yes" sounded like "YAY-ess".

He drank. The warmth in his throat felt like bliss.

"Did that taste good?" The man had a soft voice.

"Yes!" Funchess said. "I've not had a drink of water since November 4."

He shook hands with the ragged man.

"I'm Father Emil Kapaun", the man said.

"Funchess", said the young lieutenant.

"Where you from?"

"South Carolina."

"Kansas", the priest said. He then explained that he had come to the enlisted area to help GIs.

Funchess blinked. Then he realized the reason the man behaved oddly. He was hiding his little fire, the lighting of which could get him shoved into a freezing punishment hole. To come here, Kapaun had sneaked hundreds of yards carrying wood and a pan.

Funchess was a devout Methodist who concealed in his filthy clothes a small copy of the New Testament. He had not known many Catholics. This one had guts.

He thanked Kapaun. "That was the best drink I ever had in my life."

The priest grinned. Funchess felt suddenly and strangely at peace. He would remember this moment all his life. He and Kapaun would be close friends now, but for all too brief a time.

4

AS HUNDREDS DIE

*People whose ambitions are confined to the limits of earthly
things would be confounded at the beatitude on meekness.*

—Father Emil Kapaun

During that February of 1951, the Allied prisoners at Pyoktong were dying so fast on ground frozen so solid that unbur-
ied bodies lay in stacks three to four feet high, thirty to
forty yards long. Men hoarded food or stole it from the
weak, and they left the sick to die in their own defecation.

One bone-cold day, Sgt. 1st Class Bailey Gillespie lay on
the dirt floor of the Death House, the former Buddhist
monastery where the Chinese Communist guards dumped
POWs they thought were finished. The guards called it a
hospital, but everyone knew they took men there to die,
not to recover.

During the last three months, Gillespie had eaten little
more than handfuls of cracked corn or millet seed. He was
sick with pneumonia and dysentery. This combat medic for
the Twenty-Fifth Division, Twenty-Seventh Regiment knew
that dysentery was a death sentence, especially in those

conditions. Fires were prohibited, and ice congealed on the walls from his breath and that of the men with him. It was, as he heard later, at least thirty degrees below zero.

Gillespie had just turned twenty-one, and he was not a quitter. Before his capture by the Chinese on November 27, the kid from Bessemer City, North Carolina, had been a tough, good-looking guy with a square jaw and thick, wavy dark hair. His boundless energy had always served him well. He had killed men in battle—shot one enemy soldier right between the eyes. He took a grenade wound in the right hand, but didn't surrender until Chinese soldiers beat him to the ground with rifle butts.

In the prison camps, Gillespie had walked from shack to shack to treat the sick. He had browbeaten men to eat the horrible rations, to huddle for warmth and to eat snow in the absence of water. Now he was dying from dysentery.

Gillespie knew that if he gave up, the suffering would stop. But somehow in his delirium, he saw a thin, bearded man in the doorway. He was standing sideways so that the men in Gillespie's room and those in the adjoining room could hear what he had to say.

The man's voice was feeble from starvation, but his words were spoken with conviction, and that caught Gillespie's attention. Gillespie was too weak to write down what the man said, but he remembered the gist of it. The man told the sick prisoners to be true to their faith and true to those who cared about them.

Like every other POW, the man was filthy; he had a beard and long matted hair sticking out from a thick cap. His field clothes hung on him as though they enclosed a bundle of sticks.

God was with them, the man continued. They must not give up.

Then the man stuck out a skinny hand and blessed them, and Gillespie, a Protestant, recognized the Catholic Sign of the Cross. The man walked out, slow and feeble.

After a few moments, someone spoke.

"Do you know who that was?"

"No."

"That was Father Kapaun."

Gillespie lay still. He had no idea who or what Kapaun was—a priest, apparently, perhaps a chaplain. Gillespie did not know why the soldier lying near him had spoken the man's name with reverence. But something good happened to Gillespie after the priest's blessing, something he would not tell anyone about for a long time after he survived his visit to the Death House.

The suffering of that first winter was overwhelming. Many soldiers were in their teens and early twenties, not mature enough to deal with that level of misery. Kapaun never yelled at the prisoners when in their weakness they let each other down; he led by example.

When men fought over who should dig out latrines, Kapaun dug out latrines. When men argued, Kapaun mediated. When men despaired, Kapaun cracked jokes, said little prayers.

On the farm in Kansas, Kapaun's father, Enos, had taught him how to make or fix nearly anything with his hands. In the prison camps, Kapaun put those hands to good use.

POWs carried water for the camp in two leather bags hanging from a stick draped across their shoulders. The job was not only hard for the feeble men but also discouraging; by the time the leaky bags had reached their destination, they had lost half of their contents. One day the bags stopped leaking, and Dowe, curious, asked for an explanation. Some POWs told him that Kapaun had melted down an old rubber boot and made hot patches for the bags.

Life on a farm had taught Kapaun to rise early and start doing whatever needed to be done. On most mornings, he was already at work doing odd jobs before the rest of the prisoners stirred. One of his regular chores was making that hot drink he called coffee. Sometimes he made his prohibited fires with cornstalks he had scavenged from the fields and dried in the sun.

Dowe, wary at first, was surprised at how good the concoction tasted and how he felt as he drank it. Kapaun, if only briefly, made him feel civilized again, made him forget he was in a death camp.

Kapaun gave away everything he found or made, everything he had—even pieces of his clothing and portions of his rations. When he had nothing else to give, he gave blessings. Al Brooks, on wood detail one day, walked past the priest and saw him grin.

"God bless you", Kapaun said.

Brooks never forgot that or how those three words lifted him. After more than fifty-nine years, Brooks still chokes up describing that moment.

Don Slagle, a young soldier from Nebraska, went to Kapaun one day, worried about a wound festering on his leg. Men often went to Kapaun for what he gave Slagle now: reassurance.

"It'll be okay", Kapaun said.

Slagle was a Protestant, but for some reason hearing the priest say things made them seem true.

With death hanging over everyone, some men despaired. Men committed suicide by rolling away from their friends' body heat at night. Bob Wood more than once heard a fellow officer say, "I've had enough; don't bother to wake me in the morning." The next morning, that man was dead.

The men slept together spoon fashion, with cold feet clamped in the armpits of others. Even still many men died at night. One morning Funchess awoke and found the men on either side of him dead, including Dick Haugen.

Haugen had loved Kapaun so much that he had become a Catholic. The priest had baptized him in the camp. Funchess had liked Haugen, but now he stripped off the man's clothes for himself, feeling terrible as he did it.

Men were dying at such a rate, McGreevy said, that he would go to sleep among a dozen men and awaken to find two or three or four dead.

The POWs slept with corpses for days, to trick guards into giving them the dead men's rations. They ate the wretched grain even if worms wiggled in it.

Tadashi Kaneko, the headquarters' first sergeant, noticed that the young soldiers died more easily than the older men and that city folk died sooner than country folk. The soldiers from farms, and most of those the Hawaiian Kaneko called the "hillbilly soldiers from the rural South", seemed to outlast everyone. His doctor friend, Anderson, told him the guys who had grown up with privation adjusted to starvation better.

As the Americans died off by the hundreds, and as truce talks loomed, China realized the POW death toll would look embarrassing. The Chinese would feed their prisoners better.

But the extra food would come too late for many.

———#———

Father Kapaun did not plan to wait for the Chinese. He continued scrounging up food wherever he could find it and doing whatever he could to help men stay alive.

One day Wood saw Kapaun sneak into the officers' compound with a bag holding about one hundred pounds of rice. He could only wonder at how the priest had pulled off such a heist.

Another POW, David MacGhee, knew a trick or two of Kapaun's. They hunted together for rice bags in root cellars when the two slipped away from burial detail.

MacGhee teased the priest: "Isn't stealing wrong?"

"The Lord will forgive this transgression", Kapaun replied.

Men were losing frostbitten fingers or toes, the skin turning black and falling off, leaving bones as dry as sticks poking out. Kapaun brought these men and others needing immediate medical care to the doctors. To treat advanced frostbite, the doctors amputated dead bone with a butcher knife they hid from guards.

Lice multiplied overnight, congregating in armpits, inside seams, in underwear. The lice were so thick, Funchess said, that they would bleed a man to death in three days if he let them feast. Men too weak to kill them died covered with gray swarms; men too starved to care did nothing to prevent it.

But Kapaun would open the shirts of the sick and pick lice from armpits. He made it a game. "Hey, Mac," he would say, "I got seventy-five."

"Yeah?" McClain would answer. "I got ninety."

To get their minds off the incessant itching caused by lice, the POWs would play another game Kapaun invented: They would describe an elaborate exotic meal they had enjoyed in the past, vying to outdo each other in their descriptions. Among other treats described by Kapaun were those his mother made, including *kolache*, a Czech fruit-filled pastry.

Kapaun looked old at thirty-four. When GIs joked that he looked like Christ with his beard and long hair, he cringed. Yet Esensten recalled nights when weary, dispirited men came to Kapaun for whatever aid or comfort he had to give them and the full moon shone down like a spotlight on the figure of the priest.

———#———

Amid the filth one day, Wood learned that Kapaun could have avoided the perils of the Korean War. Kapaun had served in Burma and India in World War II. After that, Kapaun said, he went back to Masses and baptisms in Kansas.

"Then how did you end up here?" Wood asked.

"I volunteered."

"Father Kapaun!" Wood almost shouted. "My God, Father! Why did you come back?"

"I wanted to come back to men like these", Kapaun said. "Serving in those parishes—it didn't work out."

Then Kapaun grinned and added, "I mean, my God, Bob! Have you ever had to deal with one of those women's committees of a church Altar Society?"

———#———

Communist propaganda classes began in April; lecturers denounced Wall Street and Washington, using starvation to entice betrayal.

The guards isolated black soldiers from white, officers from enlisted men. They tried to break down the men's bonds of loyalty to each other; Kapaun fought to keep them strong, angering guards who began to badger him about Christianity.

Kapaun stood up to the Chinese indoctrinators. When he discovered that some of them had learned English in British or American missionary schools, he asked whether their Christian teachers were the deceivers that Communism claimed.

At night the chaplain led forbidden prayers; when caught, he was heckled some more. But the guards were afraid of him, McGreevy realized; when they tried to argue with Kapaun, he would quote books about God and the Church and tell them they didn't know what they were talking about. Mayo and Nardella noticed something else: The Catholic priest had captured the imagination of men from every shade of belief.

On many nights, Kapaun would gather officers after sundown on the porch of a hut and ask them to sing: "America the Beautiful" and "The Star-Spangled Banner" for the Americans; "God Save the Queen" for British officers, who had arrived in late March. To keep alive the morale and patriotism of the troops, Kapaun told the officers to sing loud enough for the enlisted men to hear. After the singing, Kapaun would give a brief sermon about Christ's insistence on forgiveness in spite of all earthly suffering.

According to Funchess and Dowe, Kapaun knew that if the men caved in to the indoctrination and the inducements to betray each other and their country, they might give up and die. But there was another reason he defied the Communists: He detested Communism. So at the lectures, Dowe said, in full view of other POWs, Kapaun told the brainwashers that they lied.

When the ground thawed a little, the men would try pitiful burials. Esensten began poking the dead men's dog tags into their mouths to aid in future identifications that he knew might never take place. Skeletal men dragged skeletal bodies to the Yalu and crossed the ice to an island. They would scratch pits two inches deep in snow, ice and rock and cover the bodies with snow and stones.

Brooks remembers a haggard Kapaun standing at the edge of the Yalu, the Manchurian breeze blowing through his beard, his long hair matted. He was blessing the dead.

Before burial Kapaun stripped the bodies, including those of men who had died in their own defecation. He would smash holes in the ice atop the river and wash the clothes in cold water; sometimes he would boil them. Men watched him spend days drying clothes, which he then gave to other prisoners.

Though he could not easily slip out of the officers' camp now, though he was growing weaker, he still made his way to the enlisted men, rallying their resistance and instilling hope.

McGreevy remembered seeing Kapaun in the enlisted men's camp at least a dozen times, gathering the POWs into little huddles.

The chaplain would tell the men to ignore the Communist "crap", which was his name for the propaganda. "Come on," he would say, "we're going to get out of here." He also encouraged them to stay alive: "Do not let your families down. Whatever else you do, keep eating."

On the camp starvation diet, McGreevy had withered from 180 plus to 100 pounds. But like Funchess, he felt a strange thing happen in the presence of Kapaun: He would forget he was starving, that the Chinese might shoot them someday soon. Two minutes in a huddle with Kapaun, and all the fear melted away.

Kapaun always addressed the men's physical needs. "Here's a little parched corn you guys can nibble on", he might say. "Is there anybody here who needs a little help? Anybody I need to look over?"

Then, after doing everything practical he could think of, he would ask: "Would anyone care to say a little prayer?"

Miller recalled how, as he was sleeping amid fourteen men in an eight-foot-by-eight-foot room, he would hear a tap on the door. A shadow would creep in, and a spark would flash in the dark. It was Kapaun with his pipe, and men desperate for a smoke would pass it around. After asking for the men's permission, Kapaun would then say a quick prayer. Then he would slip out the door, after looking both ways.

If the guards caught him, which they did sometimes, it meant time in a punishment hole, or standing on ice for hours while stripped to the skin. So Kapaun had to devise ways to evade being detected.

One evening at sundown, MacGhee came upon Kapaun carrying the two leather buckets with the stick between them over his shoulders. MacGhee asked him for a drink.

"I'm sorry, David," the priest said, "I don't have any water, just the love of Jesus Christ."

The priest tipped one bucket and then the other. They were empty, a ruse to sneak past the guards. Kapaun said the buckets hadn't fooled everybody. "I am sure that the guard knows also, and God knows about both of us."

Even under such harsh conditions, Kapaun kept his sense of humor. Years later, Mayo told author William Maher that he and Kapaun cherished a private joke that they exchanged nearly every day. Kapaun would walk past Mayo and say a sentence in Latin: "Ne illegitimi carborundum esse."

Mayo replied with the English translation: "Don't let the bastards get you down."

———

The miracle of Father Kapaun, Funchess would say later, was not just that he patched leaky buckets or stole food. It was that he rallied men to embrace life when living looked hopeless. When starvation inspired betrayals, Kapaun inspired brotherhood.

One day, as more men stole or hoarded food from each other, Kapaun walked into a hut, laid out his own food and blessed it: "Thank you, O Lord, for giving us food we can not only eat but share."

Soldiers describing the scene to Maher years later said that act put a stop to much of the stealing and hoarding. Kapaun had understood that more of the men would survive if they helped rather than victimized each other.

"The only way we could cling to life was to cling to each other", Funchess said. When he nearly died that first winter, Louis Rockwerk crushed hoarded dried peppers and garlic into the gruel to make it tastier and then fed Funchess like a baby.

The POWs grew to love Kapaun; the guards grew to hate him passionately. Funchess cringed when he saw how they abused him. They harassed him every day, for what he said, for where he walked, for how he looked.

"Where is your God now?" guards demanded.

"Right here", he replied.

Mayo one day heard a Chinese officer lecture Kapaun. "Don't ask God for your daily bread", he said. "Ask Mao Tse-tung. He's the one who provides your daily bread."

"If this is an example of God's daily bread," Kapaun replied, "then God must be a terrible baker."

Mayo watched in delight: The Chinese guards, puzzled by American sarcasm, did not know what to make of that. Was Kapaun criticizing God?

They do not know what to do with that man, Funchess thought. He deliberately said things to confound them.

But Kapaun lived on a knife's edge now; the camp commanders clearly regarded him as a threat.

"He represented a free people who refused to play along," Dowe said, "and they made him pay."

5

DEFENDER OF THE FAITH

No sincere prayer is ever wasted.

—Father Emil Kapaun

At sunrise on Easter Sunday, March 25, 1951, Kapaun startled POWs by donning his purple priest's stole and openly carrying a Catholic missal, a book with the readings and prayers for Mass and other services, borrowed from Nardella. He had talked atheist guards into letting him hold an Easter service, a favor they soon regretted.

No one there would ever forget this day. It was the most moving sight the POWs ever saw.

At sunrise, eighty officers—bearded, dirty and covered with lice—followed Kapaun up a little rise, to the cold steps of a bombed-out church. They gathered in a circle around him. Kapaun held a crude cross made from broken sticks. Except for the black eye patch, he looked to Mayo like one of the ragged apostles.

Kapaun began speaking, and his voice caught; he said he didn't have the equipment to give them a proper Mass. But then he held up his ciborium, the tiny gold container that before his capture had held Communion hosts he had placed on tongues of soldiers.

He opened Nardella's missal, and as he began to recite from it, the Christians among them realized what a risk he was now taking. He was beginning not from the Easter promise of rebirth but from the dark brutality of Good Friday.

As the guards glared, Kapaun read the Stations of the Cross, describing Christ's condemnation, torture and death. Captives who had been mocked and tormented and beaten listened as Kapaun spoke of Christ being treated in the same way.

Tears flowed.

Kapaun held up a rosary. He asked the non-Catholics to let the Catholics indulge themselves by praying the Rosary; then the Catholics knelt and recited with him the glorious mysteries of Christ rising, ascending, defying death for all time.

A voice rose in song. POW Bill Whiteside had a beautiful voice, and he raised it now to sing the Lord's Prayer, a recital that gave Esensten, the Jewish doctor, goose bumps.

Kapaun spoke. His theme: forgiveness.

He said he did not feel qualified to advise his fellow prisoners about life because, "I am not any better than you are."

Then they all sang as Kapaun had taught them: loudly so that the enlisted men could hear. Starving men reverently sang at sunrise, the same song Whiteside had sung, the Lord's Prayer.

Kapaun had rallied them all.

When guards demanded that Nardella stand before the prisoners and recite what he had learned about Communism's founders, Marx and Engels, Nardella yelled out with a straight face to fellow captives that he had learned a lot from "Marx and Engels and Amos and Andy", the last two being fools from an American radio program. POWs laughed; the guards glared.

There were now hundreds of acts of defiance in the camps every day.

Kapaun and a prisoner named William Hansen stole dysentery drugs from the Chinese dispensary and smuggled them to Esensten.

Miller began to read a pocket Bible, which one of Miller's fellow prisoners hid from the Chinese by sticking it in a bandage he had wrapped around his knee. The one place the Chinese would never search on them was under a bandage, Miller thought grimly. They let the men die of their wounds.

Funchess, in the officers' camp, had taken to reciting aloud at night from his own pocket Bible, putting his soul and his sweet Carolina accent into every tender reading. The men always asked for the Twenty-third Psalm, sometimes asking Funchess to read it fifteen or twenty times in a row. The result for Funchess was a feeling of peace.

Again and again Dowe and Funchess and the others saw Kapaun defy the Chinese propagandists until they finally gave up. He never raised his voice, but he challenged them with conviction.

It dawned on Funchess that Kapaun did this to rally the men not just to the flag but to life itself. Kapaun's actions reminded the prisoners that standing up was the opposite of giving up. A Chinese officer one day, outraged by POW defiance, told them he would shoot them all and bury them so that their "bones will forever fertilize the soil of North Korea".

There was a brief silence. Then Kapaun spoke: "What a dumb son of a bitch!"

———#———

Kapaun used colorful language when the situation seemed to warrant it, but in private moments, he would renounce his swearing, would take back some of the things he had said.

The Chinese by this time had replaced the North Korean leaders of the camps. The North Koreans had treated the Americans brutally in revenge for mauling the Koreans so badly before the Chinese entered the war. But having become embarrassed by the shocking number of POW deaths, the Chinese had taken over the administration of camps along the Yalu River.

At first the change in command meant only that the POWs starved to death at a slower rate at the hands of slightly better guards. Like the North Koreans, the Chinese hated religion, and the new camp commander, Comrade Sun, made sure Kapaun knew it.

Dowe came across Kapaun one day and was surprised to see him smiling. Kapaun stared down a road leading south.

"What are you thinking of, Father?" Dowe asked.

He was daydreaming, the priest replied, "of that happy day when the first American tank rolls down that road."

Kapaun looked at Dowe and added, "Then I'm going to catch that little so-and-so Comrade Sun and kick his ass right over the compound fence."

Another time, filled with anger at Comrade Sun, Kapaun told Dowe, "When Jesus talked about forgiving our enemies, he obviously did not have Comrade Sun in mind!"

In his cooler moments, however, Father Kapaun would, in all seriousness, remind his men of their duty, as Christians, to forgive and even to love their enemies.

⌒—#—⌐

There was at least one healing, prisoners said later.

Kapaun one day walked into a hut and took an apparently dying prisoner in his arms. Chester Osborne Jr. was one of McClain's and Dowe's closest friends, but they saw, with eyes trained by experience, that he would die soon. Kapaun cradled Osborne in his arms, laid Osborne's head on his shoulder. Kapaun then bluntly told Osborne to quit dying.

As a "precaution", he said, he would give him last rites "just in case", but he demanded that Osborne fight harder for his life. Then he prayed, for about five minutes.

Osborne rallied. His recovery surprised everybody in that hut.

Most men died quickly when they got that sick, and a lot of men got sick now. Some of the POWs had noticed during the Easter service that Father Kapaun looked ill.

⌒—#—⌐

Shortly after Easter, Kapaun came to Esensten, looking feeble, hobbling on a stick, in obvious pain. Esensten touched Kapaun's leg. Then he pulled up Kapaun's trouser and saw swelling with blue and black discoloration. He bent down and pressed a finger into a foot; the dent did not go away.

Esensten stood up angry. "You should have told me", he said. "One leg is twice the size of the other." Kapaun stood silent. Esensten asked the chaplain how long he had noticed the swelling. Two weeks, the priest said.

Esensten was not only furious but a good deal frightened; this was phlebitis, inflammation of a vein caused by a blood clot, a very serious condition. Phlebitis could be lethal to healthy people, let alone to malnourished men already weakened by disease.

The condition needed immediate treatment, Esensten said. He told Kapaun to lie down and stay down.

"No", the priest said.

⟨⟨⟨———#———⟩⟩⟩

Soon after Kapaun's visit to Esenten, Funchess awoke one night to the sound of a man being shoved into his hut. The guards had transferred Kapaun here, perhaps to separate him from McClain, another troublemaker they disliked.

Kapaun was in pain. When Funchess saw his leg, he knew sleeping in this hut would cause the priest much suffering; fourteen men slept jammed against each other and stepped on each other to get to the latrines at night.

"Would you like my spot next to the wall?" Funchess asked. Because of his injured foot, he had taken that spot weeks before. "The wall will give you protection."

For once, Kapaun did not argue with a Good Samaritan; he said yes. Funchess lay beside him in the dark, warming the priest's frail body with his own.

6

FORGIVENESS AND DEATH

In order to win the crown of heavenly glory, the saints were expected first to carry a heavy cross in life.

—Father Emil Kapaun

Over the next six weeks, the POWs in the Pyoktong prison camp began a cloaked and daring effort to save Kapaun's life.

On a rise above them stood the remains of a Buddhist monastery; the guards called it a hospital, but the POWs named it the Death House. The Chinese sometimes killed prisoners by isolating them there from food and help. The POWs knew that was where Kapaun might end up.

In April, weeks after his Easter service had irritated the guards, Kapaun's friends tried to conceal his condition. Esensten told fellow prisoners that Kapaun had a blood clot in his leg, probably caused by the many injuries he had endured in battle or in camp. Esensten and the other doctor, Anderson, explained what Kapaun needed: heat on his leg, bed rest, extra food.

So Dowe stole food for his friend. Funchess huddled with Kapaun at night to keep him warm. Men sneaked to the bombed-out church where Kapaun had given his Easter service, stole bricks, heated them in fires and gave them to Esensten; the doctor clamped the hot bricks to Kapaun's leg, which was elevated by a small trapeze made by some of the men.

Kapaun got mad and tried to get up; the doctors and the priest glared at each other. Kapaun wanted to make his prayer rounds; the doctors insisted he get well first.

Food and hot bricks turned him around. Then he got dysentery, and that quickly weakened him; he could not sleep for running to the latrine.

Funchess and a resourceful Kentuckian, Gene Shaw, intervened. Shaw sneaked out of the compound and came back with the top half of a potbellied stove he had scrounged from a bombed-out house. He and Funchess stuck one of Kapaun's homemade pans in the bottom and told Kapaun he now had a private commode; no running to the latrine necessary.

When they saw that Kapaun was too weak to mount it himself, they lifted him there—then wiped his bottom for him. This deeply embarrassed Kapaun, but Funchess told him he had seen him do the same for others.

Esensten now hatched a daring plan. He talked to men all over the camp. The result was an outbreak of fake POW dysentery throughout the officers' compound. Chinese doctors saw dozens of men with "diarrhea". They gave medicine, and the men smuggled it to Esensten, who gave it to Kapaun—who got better.

But the disease had taken its toll. At night Funchess could see Kapaun fight spasms of pain. Advanced starvation causes pain deep in the bones, reducing soldiers to tears. It also caused Kapaun's and Dowe's genitals to swell, making it painful to move.

Even in this weakened state, Kapaun reached out to comfort others, and men came to him for his blessing.

Lying beside the priest one night, Funchess confided in Kapaun. The priest had just turned thirty-five; Funchess was only twenty-four, a boy in comparison.

"I don't think I'm going to make it, Father", Funchess said. "I can hardly walk on my foot; it's going to get an infection. I'm starving."

"No, no," Kapaun said, "you're going to get better; you're going to get out of here. So you just walk on that foot."

Funchess asked about forgiveness.

"Of course we should forgive them", Kapaun said of their captors. "We should not only forgive our enemies but love them too."

But they shot wounded soldiers, Funchess said. They abused prisoners.

It doesn't matter, Kapaun said. "If we fail to forgive, we're rejecting our own faith."

———

Incredibly now, with barely enough strength to breathe, with the POWs trying to conceal him from guards bent on finishing him off, Kapaun rallied enough to help Funchess make pots and pans.

One day Funchess, also a farmer's son, had asked Kapaun, "You're the only guy in camp who can take a square piece of roofing tin and make a pan that doesn't leak out of all four corners. How do you do that?"

"You got to know when to crimp an edge inside and when to bend outside", Kapaun answered. He was lying on the dirt floor, with barely enough strength to open his eyes. "I could show you", he said.

"No," Funchess said, "you rest."

Funchess left for a few minutes and came back with pencil and scrap paper. For hours, the farm boy from Kansas dictated detailed instructions to the farm boy from South Carolina, who wrote it all down. Funchess at last held the paper before Kapaun's eyes.

"I think you got it!" Kapaun said.

After that, other POWs made watertight pans.

Kapaun could barely breathe because he had come down with pneumonia. Esensten and other officers demanded sulfa powder. Guards said there wasn't any. The Americans demanded that the Chinese do more to help Kapaun. "Let God save him", the Chinese replied. "He's a man of God."

Kapaun made feeble attempts to talk. A POW next door wanted to convert to Catholicism; Kapaun spoke to him. Felix McCool came to confess; Kapaun sat up and blessed him in Latin, then sank back, delirious.

"I am going to die", Kapaun told McCool.

Esensten refused to accept this. With Kapaun's determination to live, he said, the priest had a good chance of recovery, provided his friends kept him warm, fed and rested. And Kapaun did begin to recover.

In late May 1951, when the breezes of spring refreshed the faces of men even in that desolate place, Anderson thought Kapaun was going to make it.

But then the Chinese came. They came brusquely and rudely through the hut door. Backed by a squad of Chinese soldiers with rifles, Comrade Sun waved his pistol in the air and fired it. He must have heard about Kapaun's recovery and had decided to stop it.

The guards laid a stretcher down and pointed at Kapaun.

"No!" Funchess said. "He's fine and stays with us."

"He goes!" Sun said.

Things escalated. The men first argued then yelled threateningly at the guards: "Leave him!"

Emaciated prisoners—Protestants, Jews, agnostics, atheists—hobbled out of the hut, calling for help. More men, so weak they could barely stand, hurried to where voices got louder by the moment. Esensten and Anderson tried to reason with the guards.

Let us continue his care; he is recovering, Esensten pleaded.

The guards glared. "We'll take care of him", Sun said. The guards shouted at what was now a mob of prisoners: "He will do better with us!"

The Chinese stood their ground, rifles in hand. More men crowded around, and Funchess saw one of the skeletal Americans shove a Chinese rifleman; the rifleman shoved back.

The Chinese did not yet aim their rifles at the POWs, but they grew nervous. There was more shoving, until a voice spoke from the floor.

At first, Funchess didn't hear it. But then men pointed to Kapaun. He was so weak he could barely speak; he was in so much pain his face was contorted.

"I'll go", he said. "Don't get into any trouble over me." Men sobbed like children.

Kapaun handed his gold ciborium to Mayo.

"Tell them I died a happy death", he said.

He would keep his purple stole and his little vials of holy oils, he added; perhaps he could help in the hospital.

He told a story from the Old Testament book of Maccabees: A king threatened to kill seven sons and their mother unless they all forsook God. With tears, the mother encouraged her sons to keep the faith, but they were tears of joy. She watched as each of her sons in turn was tortured and murdered. Then she too was killed.

Nardella bent down when Kapaun beckoned.

"You know the prayers, Ralph", Kapaun said. He handed back Nardella's missal and added, "Keep holding the services. Don't let them make you stop."

Kapaun told Nardella to take care of the men and stick to the principles of his faith—"all of them".

Phil Peterson, who had helped Kapaun lead the Rosaries, put a hand on Kapaun's arm. "I'm terribly sorry", he said.

"You're sorry for me?" Kapaun responded. "I am going to be with Jesus Christ. And that is what I have worked for all my life. And you say you're sorry for me? You should be happy for me."

Kapaun beckoned to another prisoner. "When you get back to Jersey," he told him, "you get that marriage straightened out. Or I'll come down from heaven and kick you in the ass."

Dowe by this time was sobbing.

"Don't take it hard, Mike", Kapaun said. "I'm going where I've always wanted to go. And when I get up there, I'll say a prayer for all of you."

The Americans bluntly told the guards they would carry Kapaun themselves. The POW leaders asked for volunteers, and the men within earshot nearly fought each other for the honor.

Four POWs, including Nardella and Wood, placed Kapaun on the stretcher.

Anderson, the doctor who had taken equal risks on the battlefield with Kapaun before they were captured, looked him over one last time and marveled. He and Esensten knew better than anybody the terrible pain he was in.

Dowe, heartbroken and furious, realized he was witnessing a murder, a martyrdom. Kapaun's fever had broken, and he seemed to be recovering. The Chinese clearly wanted to stop that.

Dowe knew where the Chinese were taking the priest—up the hill, but not to the hospital where they fed sick prisoners, but to the nearby shed filled with maggots and feces, the Death House. They isolated the sickest men there and let them die of thirst.

Apart from the doctors, no one looking at Kapaun now would detect the pain the priest was masking. His face: serene. His voice: calm. Anderson saw Kapaun smile and wave to the men who watched as he was taken away, men bent with grief.

A Turkish officer named Fezi Bey watched the priest in awe. He and the other Turks were tough men, Muslims who had known little about Christianity before their capture. They respected Kapaun deeply.

The stretcher bearers reached the entrance to the Death House; Kapaun raised a hand and blessed the guards. Tears poured down Wood's cheeks.

Kapaun looked at Nardella. In heaven, he said, he would pray for Nardella's return home.

Then he glanced around at the waiting Chinese. "Forgive them, for they know not what they do", he said.

He looked at a Chinese officer and said, "Forgive me."

His friends set him down where several other prisoners lay dead or dying. Wood walked into an adjoining ward and pleaded with the sick prisoners there: "Father is in a bad way; try to help him if you can." But they looked too weak to help anyone.

Wood, prodded by the guards, walked back to the compound, so distraught he could barely see.

"My God," he thought, "if God is taking this man, what has he got in store for the rest of us?"

Then he pushed down that thought, telling himself that Kapaun would never think like that.

Kapaun lasted two days without food or water. Then he died.

And that was the end of him. Or so the guards hoped.

———

All over the officers' compound, men sat for days in shock. And then, little by little, unusual things began to happen.

Soon after Kapaun's death, in the ward adjacent to where he had taken his last breath, gravely ill McGreevy crawled away from the spot on the floor where the Chinese had abandoned him to die.

The former football player from Cumberland, Maryland, knew that he needed to get his leg muscles moving or they would atrophy, and then he would be even further beyond any chance of recovery.

He made his way to a corner where he could place his big hands on two walls at once. He took a deep breath, gathered his feet and said a prayer he had never prayed before.

A Catholic, McGreevy had been taught that, when all hope seemed lost, one could pray to a saint, a person in heaven who had the ear of God. McGreevy prayed now to a man who fit that description. For all anyone knows, McGreevy was the first person to say this particular prayer: "Father Kapaun, help me."

And then, for the first time in weeks, McGreevy stood up.

———

Down the hill from the Death House, in the huts of Pyoktong, Funchess continued to defy the camp guards by reading the Twenty-third Psalm every night to fellow prisoners. Funchess had read the psalm to himself after Kapaun died; now he read it to other men who also had loved the priest.

In another hut, Mayo hid Kapaun's gold ciborium so the guards could not confiscate it. Nardella led prisoners in saying the Rosary in forbidden religious services.

Little by little, as the first shock of Father Kapaun's death wore off, men began to tell and retell the stories about him: his friendship, his jokes, his deeds, his faith.

That generous man, who died alone, who lay now in an unmarked grave, had never told them what to do. He had never pushed religion on them. But he had nevertheless taught them to stand up for themselves, to help each other and to forgive.

Not long after the priest's death peace negotiations started, and the Chinese finally began to feed the POWs a little better. The survivors rallied and pulled themselves together, telling each other that the man who had died for them deserved a gift in return—

Their survival.

7

KAPAUN'S CROSS

He died because he loved and pitied us. He died that we might live.

—Father Emil Kapaun

The legend of Father Kapaun and the quest to see him properly honored began in September 1953, as soon as Communist guards released POWs after the Korean War ended.

A little band of fierce-looking Americans, with the balding and blunt-talking Nardella at their head, took with them out of the camp Kapaun's gold ciborium and a rugged wooden crucifix, a formidable sculpture only an inch shy of four feet tall.

Nardella and the others had risked their safety in this final act of defiance. The guards had wanted to confiscate these items, but Nardella had threatened to stay in North Korea, embarrassing their captors.

The determined group walked directly to the foreign correspondents who were covering the prisoner release and said they had a world-class story to tell. Within hours, wire services were transmitting accounts of Father Kapaun, along with photos of Nardella, Joseph O'Connor and Felix McCool holding the crucifix.

The men told how Father Kapaun had at least two tobacco pipes shot out of his mouth as he dragged wounded men off battlefields. They said he saved men on a death march, washed the underwear of the sick, made water pans out of roofing tin and stole food.

"Maybe I shouldn't say it," O'Connor said in a wire-service story that appeared in the *Wichita Beacon*, "but he was the best food thief we had."

The stories appeared in papers around the world and made Kapaun an international hero.

The articles quoted O'Connor explaining how Kapaun celebrated Mass under fire, spreading bread and wine on the hood of his jeep, never flinching at explosions.

"I am a Jew," Esensten told the reporters, "but I feel deeply the greatness of the man, regardless of religion."

Anderson returned to his home in Long Beach, California, and gave an extended interview to newspaper reporters. A hero himself—he had refused, along with Kapaun, to escape from the Battle of Unsan in order to tend the wounded—the doctor declined to talk about his own role. Instead, he focused the attention on Kapaun.

"He was a man without personal motives," Anderson said, "without any regard for his personal safety or comfort. He simply did what his moral and ethical code told him was his duty. He totally disregarded danger. He felt that as long as God wanted him to go on caring for the battle victims, nothing would happen to him.

"Father Kapaun's perfect peace of mind was a tremendous influence on the morale of the troops before and after capture", Anderson continued. "With just a few words of assurance, and with his constant example of devotion to the men's welfare, he was especially effective among those whom imprisonment had demoralized."

Anderson related the most Christ-like action he saw the priest do. Before Kapaun was taken to a place where he would be left to die, in the company of the men he loved he "asked the Chinese officer in charge—a snaky-looking and -acting person who could provoke only revulsion—he asked this fellow to forgive him for whatever wrongs he might have done him.

"I couldn't understand why Father Kapaun would ask this fellow's forgiveness," Anderson reflected, "until I figured out that after all, it hadn't been easy for him not to hate his captors.

"He is a man I cannot even think about without a marked feeling of reverence."

To honor Kapaun, Anderson explained, he was raising money to fulfill a task the chaplain had intended to perform. The idea came from Nardella, who said Kapaun had confided in him that when he got home he would give $1,000 in back pay to the poor in his Kansas parish.

———※———

The tributes devastated Kapaun's mother, father and brother. The stories that trumpeted his heroism also confirmed that Emil was dead. Only recently had the army broken the news to the family in a letter from Maj. Gen. William E. Bergin, who wrote:

> I sincerely regret that this message must carry so much sorrow into your home, and I hope that in time you may find sustaining comfort in knowing that he served his country honorably. My deepest sympathy is extended to you in your bereavement.

Kapaun's parents struggled to maintain their composure as the stories of their son spread and as reporters started coming to the farmhouse door wanting information about their son. Many Americans, including Kapaun's fellow soldiers and his bishop, were already coupling his name with the title "saint".

Emil Kapaun's life was so simple before the war that any reporter asking about him would learn this: his early years were anything but remarkable.

As a boy he rode to church on a bicycle, getting off to pick flowers for the sanctuary before serving as an altar boy at Mass. He was the only kid around who never got his knuckles rapped by the nuns who taught at his school.

While a young priest he delighted the children in the parish. They had almost no sports equipment, so he taught them the soccer he had learned in the seminary. When in catechism class Millie Vinduska mispronounced "Saint Thomas Aquinas" as "Saint Thomas Equinox", he endeared himself to the students by struggling visibly to contain his gentle laughter.

His problems were those of any young priest, especially one who had grown up in the parish. Although the people of Pilsen now regarded Kapaun as a saint, when he had walked among them, some had struggled to accept him as a priest. Some of them could not abide the son of a local farmer as their representative of the Deity.

Millie Vinduska remembers an elder Czech dismissing him: "He's just a kid!" Her fellow Czechs could be stubborn, irritating and crabby, Vinduska said; there was friction.

Kapaun wrote his bishop, begging to be sent as a chaplain to the United States Army:

When I was ordained, I was determined to "spend myself" for God. I was determined to do that cheerfully, no matter in what circumstances I would be placed or how hard a life I would be asked to lead. This is why I volunteered for the army and that is why today I would a thousand times rather be working, deprived of all ordinary comforts, being a true "Father" to all my people, than to be living in a nice, comfortable place but with my conscience telling me that I am an obstacle to many.

So his bishop traded the Czech-speaking Kapaun for the Czech-speaking priest in the central Kansas town of Timken.

It was all so ordinary, including the pettiness of churchgoers finding fault with the pastors who served them. "No prophet is accepted in his own country", Jesus once ruefully said after an unpleasant visit to his own hometown.

There is one story from the priest's childhood, however, that stood out, because it showed Kapaun was the same incredibly resourceful person at age six or seven that he was at age thirty-four.

Kapaun's mother milked the family cow and taught her son how to do the job. One day, according to neighbor Amelia Vinduska, when Kapaun was first assigned by his mother to take over the milking, the cow refused to cooperate. So the boy went to the house, put on his mother's dress and fooled the cow into standing still.

Kapaun's old friends, after the first wave of soldiers and reporters had told them of his deeds, were all thrilled and proud. But when reporters talked to his mother, Bessie told them she had opposed her son's return to the army.

"But he said the boys needed him more than we did," she said, "and he went."

Kapaun would have been upset had he known the risks his friends would take to honor his memory.

Back in the POW camp before the war ended, Mayo had hidden Kapaun's ciborium, but the guards took it anyway. Weeks later, Mayo, Nardella and other POWs nearly rioted when a prisoner saw the camp commander's four-year-old daughter throwing the ciborium in the air and catching it. Nardella demanded it; the Chinese refused to give it back until the war's end.

A few weeks after Kapaun died, a Marine Corps fighter pilot, Maj. Jerry Fink, was brought to the POW camp. He heard a lot about Father Kapaun from the prisoners, even from the Muslim Fezi Bey, who told Fink that Kapaun had awed all the Turks.

"He is not of my religion, but he is a man of God", Fezi said.

Fink was a Jew with little interest in Christianity. He was also an artist, a fix-it man and a patriot. He hated the Communist guards who had beaten him several times.

Fink and Nardella were kindred spirits about resistance to the enemy, so when Nardella said he wanted a shrine to honor Kapaun even though it would defy the guards, Fink vowed to do something profound.

What happened next became the next chapter in the Kapaun legend: the Jewish warrior carving a sculpture of the crucified Christ.

Fink spent weeks picking over firewood. He selected pieces of scrub oak for the cross and fine-grained cherry wood for the body.

Other prisoners, including Mayo's buddy Phil Peterson, showed Fink how to tear up old GI boots, removing the steel arches. Fink and Peterson spent weeks filing steel on rocks until they had sharp blades. Fink also made a chisel out of a broken drainpipe.

The Marine pilot spent months carving a 47-inch-by-28-inch cross. He carved a two-foot-long body and a bearded face, which many said looked surprisingly like that of Kapaun, whom Fink had never met.

The artist twisted radio wire to make a crown of thorns. He sneaked up to the building of the camp commander, smashed a window and picked up a few shards of glass. These he used to sand the sculpture smooth.

Guards demanded to know the identity of Fink's sculpture.

"Abraham Lincoln", Fink lied. The guards regarded Lincoln as a nonreligious kindred spirit, so they were fooled into letting this go.

When at last they realized the figure was Christ, some guards spat at it; others threw Fink into a punishment hole. But they seemed afraid to touch the sculpture.

Years later, when Fink visited Kapaun's friends and family in Kansas, he talked of hate. "I can still bring up the hate. It's what kept me going."

But what made him carve the crucifix was the story of a man who rejected hate, who told all the Jerry Finks of the world to love their enemies. Fink did not emulate that idea—but he risked his life to honor it.

"If the meek shall inherit the earth, it will be because people like Father Kapaun willed it to them", Fink told reporters in Wichita. "I am a Jew, but that man will always live in my heart."

Visits by Fink and others brought some peace to the Kapauns; but it was not enough to compensate for the loss of their son.

Bessie was brought to tears every time reporters called. She would sometimes play a recording of Emil's voice giving

a sermon over Armed Forces Radio in Tokyo not long before
he shipped out for Korea. She would listen to her son talk
about saints, about how they were tested. And she would
cry.

When reporters asked Enos about Emil, the old farmer
looked at the ground.

"You know," he said, "since he is gone, I am just no
good."

———✕———

Bailey Gillespie, who had survived the Death House, came
home after the war and soon married. He and Joy dated
only two weeks between meeting and tying the knot.

For a long time, Gillespie told Joy nothing about his experiences in Korea. But he carried the war with him. At night,
with Joy sleeping beside him, Gillespie would scream in
the darkness. He screamed for years. Sometimes, in the grip
of those nightmares, he would grab Joy and yell: "Hit that
ditch! Hit that ditch!"

One day Joy suggested to her husband that he talk about
the war; maybe it would help. Then he told her about the
battles and the POW camp where hundreds of men died.
He told how sometimes the feeble soldier who helped Gillespie
carry a body to the Yalu River for burial on Monday would
be the dead man he carried to the burial on Tuesday.

Sometimes, he said, the lice multiplied so fast that Gillespie
would find a sick soldier coated white with thousands of
pests; he was too weak to pick them off himself. It was so
cold that nobody took his boots off. Gillespie didn't take
off his boots from November to April. When he did, his
feet swelled, and he could not get his boots back on.

He told Joy about the thin man who had come to visit
the sick in the Death House on a bone-chilling day in

February 1951. The man had said a few words, and then something good happened.

The little heartfelt sermon strengthened Gillespie's faith in God. It encouraged Gillespie to stay alive. He hung on the next day, and the next, even as the dysentery weakened him.

He looked up at one point and thought that he was looking up from the bottom of a grave; a white light appeared at his feet. But the words of that thin man still sounded in his mind, giving Gillespie hope, and he refused to go to the light that beckoned him to leave this world.

The fever went away, and the chills, and the dysentery. Gillespie forced himself to eat and drink. A month later, he did something few men ever did: He walked out of the Death House.

Two and a half years later, he walked out of the prison camp.

Over the next six decades, he and Joy had children and grandchildren; they have two great-grandsons.

After Gillespie began to talk about his war experiences, Joy wrote down his stories and helped get them published as *Korean War Remembered: Prisoner of War, 1013 Days in Hell*. She wanted the great-grandsons to know who and what their great-grandfather was.

God saved his life, Gillespie said, but Kapaun gave him a boost when he needed it. If not for Kapaun's visit, he would have given up, and there would be no great-grandchildren walking around.

At the time, Gillespie had not even known who that thin man was. Or what he was.

It was much later—many years later—when Gillespie learned the identity of that man. And when he did, he said something a little unusual for a Protestant like himself.

He said Emil Kapaun was a saint.

———//———

Although some Catholics saw Kapaun's potential for canonization, for decades they did little to push it.

Wichita Bishop Mark Carroll, Kapaun's boss when he
served as a priest in Pilsen, told reporters that Kapaun's sanc-
tity was evident soon after POWs had revealed his heroism.
The diocese began collecting information; books were
contemplated.

Some in the Church's hierarchy decided that because
Kapaun was a military chaplain, the Archdiocese for the
Military Services should lead the investigation.

Decades passed. Eventually Bishop Carroll's successors realized that the understaffed chaplain service never pressed the
cause for sainthood to conclusion; the Wichita Diocese
decided to take over.

———//———

The POWs never stopped seeking recognition for their
hero.

Kapaun's friends, including McClain, Mayo, Dowe and
Wood repeatedly went to Wichita and Pilsen; they testified
on tape, signed affidavits and wrote polite, insistent letters
to both military and Church officials.

They asked the military to review whether Kapaun should
receive the Medal of Honor.

A fellow Eighth Cavalry soldier who was awarded that
medal said Kapaun should have received it too.

"Maybe they thought a guy who didn't carry a gun
shouldn't win the Medal of Honor", Tibor Rubin said.

———//———

No POW did more for Kapaun's memory than Dowe. Over six decades he was a diplomatic and determined advocate for his friend. But he very nearly did not survive to tell the tale.

While still in the POW camp, Dowe seethed with anger for two and a half years after Kapaun's death. He had hated Communism already; and after Communist guards murdered his friend, his hatred burned hotter than ever, fueling an almost reckless defiance.

He watched with grim satisfaction when the guards, one year after Kapaun's death, refused to let the POWs hold a service in his honor.

"It meant they were still afraid of him", Dowe said.

When peace negotiations started in June 1951, the Chinese fed the POWs somewhat better, but they moved several of their worst troublemakers, including Nardella and Dowe, to another camp where they could control them better.

There Nardella continued the weekly improvised Catholic services begun by Kapaun.

Dowe, still grieving but no longer starving, wrote songs for a couple of POW musicals he produced. The guards allowed these diversions—and regretted it.

Dowe's lyrics included salty insults aimed at their captors. The prisoners managed to hide these creations from the guards during rehearsals, but after the performances the guards threw Dowe into the punishment hole.

The last satirical song Dowe wrote was memorized by the prisoners, who sang it aloud in the trucks on their way to the prisoner exchange after the war. The act nearly cost Dowe his life. At Panmunjom, with freedom only hours away, guards apprehended Dowe, along with half a dozen other offenders, tried them and condemned them as enemies of Communism. They told them they would never leave North Korea.

Decades later, Dowe could still sing from memory the lyrics that had almost cost him his freedom:

They say now the treatment was lenient.
Of this we're no longer in doubt.
They beat us and kicked us
and laughed at our sickness
and said that we'd never get out.

That was disrespectful enough. But then came this, which looked innocent on paper until the POWs performing it used a four-letter obscenity instead of "bless":

Bless them all.
Bless them all.
The long and the short and the tall.
Bless all the letters we never did get
and all the daikons [turnips] we'll never forget.
Now we're saying goodbye to them all—
Bless them all.

That night Dowe made his way to a latrine. He dropped down into the foul smell, crawled the length of the latrine out of sight and hid. The next day, he climbed onto the last truck of prisoners crossing to freedom. When a guard with a clipboard tried to stop him, Dowe pointed at the clipboard and said his name, as though it were on the list, and kept walking.

Had the Chinese known what the man who was escaping would become, they might have tried more frantically to stop him. Dowe became a nuclear physicist and worked with weaponry.

But the other troublemakers condemned with Dowe the day before—no one ever saw them again.

Kapaun's subtle leadership would intrigue Dowe for the rest of his life. In coming years he would meet generals, members of Congress, CEOs, winners of the Medal of Honor and leading scientists. But he said he seldom saw any leader like Kapaun: "The greatest man I ever knew."

Dowe was happy when he learned that Kapaun had been awarded the Distinguished Service Cross, the army's second-highest honor, for his deeds in combat. But Dowe, though he respected military hierarchy, did not think the award was enough for Kapaun.

There seemed to be a rule in the military at the time that prevented awarding the Medal of Honor for actions performed in a POW camp. Dowe did not think this rule was fair, because it did not take into account the heroism that is sometimes exhibited by POWs, who are often subjected to the most inhumane treatment imaginable.

It wasn't right, thought Dowe, that a man who had sacrificed himself in order to save and inspire hundreds of others, and had been killed by the enemy for doing so, could not be considered for a Medal of Honor. He decided that he would right this wrong, and soon he was in a position to do so.

Months after his release, Dowe went to work at the Pentagon, where he told stories about the North Korean prisoner-of-war camps and about the chaplain named Emil Kapaun.

Army officers, impressed, introduced Dowe to Harold Martin, an editor at one of the nation's most respected media giants of that time, the *Saturday Evening Post*. Martin, a gifted writer, helped Dowe write a story that on January 16, 1954, brought an extended account of Kapaun's heroism to a worldwide audience. The two men wrote:

He was a priest of the Church, and a man of great piety.
But there was nothing ethereal about him, nothing soft or
unctuous or holier-than-thou . . . outwardly he was all GI,
tough of body, rough of speech sometimes, full of the wry
humor of the combat soldier. In a camp where men had to
steal or starve, he was the most accomplished food thief of
them all. In a prison whose inmates hated their communist
captors with a bone-deep hate, he was the most unbending
enemy of communism, and when they tried to brainwash
him, he had the guts to stand up to them and tell them to
their faces that they lied.

Dowe served Kapaun and country. He worked for President Eisenhower's presidential commission that formulated
a new Armed Forces Code of Conduct based in part on
the Korean War POW experience. He became a nuclear
physicist, doing important work with strategic weaponry,
including the Star Wars program studied by the Reagan
administration. All the while, he told people about his great
friend.

In spring 1954, while still recovering from his prison
camp ordeals, Dowe stood in for Kapaun's parents when
the U.S. military honored Capt. Emil Kapaun as Chaplain
of the Year in a ceremony at National Memorial Park in
Falls Church, Virginia. He wrote Enos and Bessie immediately after.

It was indeed a pleasure to have been permitted to accept
for you, in your absence, this award to the greatest man I
have ever known. You and I and the many others who knew
and loved him realize the insufficiency of words to describe
your great loss.

Throughout our history great men like your son, by their
sacrifices, have built and preserved our country. Father
Kapaun died fighting for the things he loved and believed

in. I shall always consider it a privilege to have known so
great a priest, so great a soldier and so great an American
as your son.

In 1955 actor James Whitmore played Kapaun in a national
television show, *The Good Thief*, wearing an eye patch, stealing food, praying in violation of camp rules. Some script
lines came right from Dowe's story in the *Post*.

These moves were only the first in a campaign that Dowe
would carry on for the next six decades.

———*//*———

The stories of Kapaun's courage and generosity resonated
everywhere.

Nardella, when he got a hero's welcome in New Jersey,
was surprised to learn that local newspapers and citizens
had already raised the $1,000 Nardella had said Father Kapaun
wanted to give to the Pilsen poor fund. Before Nardella
took the money to Kansas, that fund would grow much
larger—to $8,300.

In May 1957 Cardinal Francis Spellman, friend to popes
and one of the most prominent religious figures in the United
States, came to Wichita to honor Father Kapaun. The archbishop of New York sat with the bishop of Wichita as they
named a Catholic high school after him. The seed money
for the school had come from Nardella's fund.

At dinner that night, the two churchmen heard impas-
sioned speeches.

"Father Kapaun's courage had the softness of velvet and
the strength of iron", Mayo told them.

"More than a man," said Anderson, "a hero and a saint."

Nardella told them that he had nearly died one day from
beriberi and pneumonia. "It was the lowest point in my

life", Nardella said, until Kapaun came to his hut. "Before you have an Easter you must have a Good Friday", Kapaun had told him.

But the dinner showed how fast the legacies of even great people can fade.

Kapaun's brother, Eugene, as his wife related later, was mystified to hear Carroll, the priest's own bishop, and Spellman, the military vicar, mispronounce his and his brother's last name, saying "KAYpin" instead of "kuhPAWN".

For years after, Eugene—who served as a maintenance man in the school that bore his own name—tried to correct people. He told Dowe later that he kept correcting people until he realized no one listened. Eventually even people in Pilsen said "KAYpin".

The Wichita Diocese as early as the late 1950s was handing out Father Kapaun prayer cards, one of which went to a two-story house in the southern part of the city. There, where two parents and nine kids competed for two bathrooms, Sylvester and Frances Hotze raised a son who knew about Kapaun because his parents had taped the prayer card to the bathroom mirror; John Hotze saw Kapaun every time he brushed his teeth.

Later, after Hotze was ordained, he asked to serve Kapaun's parish in Pilsen, an hour's drive north of Wichita. Hotze had felt called.

By 2001, when the diocese decided to step up efforts to investigate Kapaun's candidacy for sainthood, Hotze became the logical choice to gather information on his behalf for the Vatican.

He began to call old soldiers. They were glad to help him.

Kapaun's war buddies had never given up pressing his case. Over decades, they persisted in telling his story, suggesting the Medal of Honor, claiming their friend belonged in the ranks of saints.

Hotze traveled. He taped interviews with Dowe, Funchess, Miller, McGreevy and others. In 2009 they heard hopeful news from the U.S. Army. It made their skin tingle.

8

DEFINING A MIRACLE

Perfection is acquired through our efforts, and if we try to become saints, someday we will be saints.

— Father Emil Kapaun

Chase Kear does not seem at first glance to be the poster boy for a Vatican investigation involving sainthood. He chews a little dip, hits targets at turkey shoots, listens to country music when he rolls. In his Facebook profile photo he dresses the part of a half-naked bandito in a sombrero. He's a self-described redneck; he was foolish and drunk and stupid at times in the past, he says, although he has been less so since his accident.

He takes comfort in knowing that Jesus reached out to sinners, because a sinner Chase Kear sometimes is. Jesus loves him anyway, he believes.

Kear's life changed when it should have ended on October 2, 2008. The pole-vaulter on the Hutchinson Community College track team felt something go slack in the flex of his pole as he turned upside down in midair. He overshot the mat.

The impact on the ground caved in the right side of his skull. He stopped breathing; paramedics stuck a tube down his throat. His eyeballs stared sightless in different directions. His limp arms and legs would not move when paramedics jabbed them.

"He was dead", family doctor Joe Davison said later.

At the hospital surgeons sawed off the right side of his skull to relieve the brain's swelling.

Family and friends began chanting Hail Marys, Our Fathers and a prayer asking for the intercession of Father Emil Kapaun on behalf of their stricken loved one.

The Kears barely knew who Kapaun was. But reciting the Kapaun prayer before daily Mass is what Catholics do in Colwich. It's a wisp of a town northwest of Wichita, surrounded by wheat fields. The diocese has handed out Kapaun prayer cards for the sick for decades.

Davison, when he learned how bad Chase's injury was, steeled himself to comfort a grieving family and secondarily to plan for long-term care. If Chase survived, he would surely be an invalid needing diapers. Other doctors made the same predictions to Chase's parents, Paul and Paula.

Paula said they should pray. They and their friends said thousands of prayers asking for Kapaun's intercession. After that something amazing happened. Doctors called it impossible.

———— # ————

Kapaun's comrades revere him to this day. Some of them pray to him.

Many of the POWs suffered terribly after the war, and their memories of Father Kapaun have brought them comfort.

Funchess accidentally hit his wife in bed one night in Clemson, South Carolina, as he thrashed in his sleep. For decades he had nightmares about staring up at hundreds of Chinese aiming rifles at him. Another dream involved being forced back into the camp; in the dream, he ransacked his house looking for nail and hair clippers and other comforts he had lacked as a POW.

Funchess says not a day goes by when he does not think of Kapaun.

In Pulaski, New York, Joyce Miller woke up one night to find her husband, Herb, climbing the wall above the bed, trying to run from guards coming to shoot him.

Miller has a bronze replica of the Pilsen statue of Father Kapaun with a wounded soldier. It stands in a place of honor in his living room.

A few years back, Miller was startled, in going through some old things, to come across the brown, fragile piece of paper on which he had scribbled instructions from Kapaun on how to make leak-proof pans out of bomb-twisted roofing tin. He sent the paper to Father Hotze in Wichita, who placed it with the other Kapaun relics in the diocesan files.

For some of the former POWs, their thoughts of Kapaun also include prayers to him. Dowe, who lives in Houston, has prayed to the soul of his friend every night since he died.

Lawrence Donovan, who had heard Kapaun tell the starving officers at Sombakol to let the enlisted men eat first, said he has prayed to Kapaun every night since the war.

He was sick and on dialysis at his home in Pittsburgh, Pennsylvania, when contacted for the newspaper version of this story early in 2011. The local priest was coming around on Sundays and giving him Holy Communion in his bed.

McGreevy, who revived in the prison-camp ward near the Death House while praying to Kapaun, still prays to him.

"I will say an Our Father and a Hail Mary", he said. "Then I pray to him: 'Father Kapaun, thank you so much for giving us the courage to keep going.'"

McGreevy went home to Cumberland, Maryland, after the war and married Marian, the prettiest girl in town. He worked for the Postal Service, raised children and regained enough health to run marathons, including in Boston and New York.

Marian died five years ago; McGreevy still cries. He never cried in the prison camps.

At POW reunions, he and Brooks—the prisoner Kapaun blessed one day while on wood detail—grin as they tell other former POWs at the dinner table, "Whatever you do, keep eating." It is a wry salute to the priest who hounded them to stay alive.

Funchess, Dowe and Wood all kept the brass spoons they used when they ate those tiny meals of millet and cracked corn in Pyoktong. Wood proudly hung his spoon on his living-room wall.

His Silver Star, on the other hand, he stored in a dresser drawer. When a journalist asked in 2009 to photograph his medal for bravery, Wood paused to remember where he had put it. He had to search several drawers before he found it.

Kapaun's friends left their children legacies involving more than spoons. Patrick Schuler, a young soldier who served as Kapaun's driver, framed Raymond Skeehan's iconic photograph of the priest saying an outdoor Mass before an altar on the hood of his jeep. The photo hung in Schuler's house for years before he told his son Tom that the kneeling soldier pictured with Kapaun was himself.

Patrick Schuler refused to go to Fourth of July celebrations because the explosions of firecrackers and fireworks bothered him. He seldom talked about the war before he died in 1987, Tom Schuler said. But when he did, he always mentioned Kapaun, saying he was an example of how a man could lead others even if he wasn't an officer of high rank.

In the 1970s, when Tom Schuler became an officer in the Marine Corps, his father reminded him of what he had said about Kapaun.

"Remember what leadership is", Patrick Schuler told his son. "It's not about the rank; it's about the man."

Some of those who served and suffered beside Kapaun in Korea were so elderly by 2012, when the manuscript for this book was completed, that they were losing hope that they would see either a White House ceremony for the Medal of Honor or a sainthood ceremony at Saint Peter's in Rome.

The decision-making gears of the Roman Catholic Church and the U.S. government move too slowly for Kapaun's friends who would like him to receive in their lifetimes the ultimate recognition they think he deserves. That is one reason they agreed to be interviewed by the *Wichita Eagle*.

Starting in June 2009, twelve elderly POWs began to tell their stories to the *Eagle*, so that the facts about Kapaun could be recorded for history. Most of them, still sick at heart at what they had seen of war and cruelty, would never have talked about the war to anyone.

McGreevy had never told his own children about how he had fought in combat and nearly died from inhumane treatment in a POW camp. When his daughters read about all this in the *Eagle*'s story in 2009, they were shocked.

The only reason he talked to reporters, McGreevy said, was to tell the world what that priest had done to save his life.

When Chase Kear hit the ground, his brain rattled inside his skull in the same way a clapper bangs inside a ringing bell.

Doctors told Kear's parents that their son probably would die. The trauma to the brain likely caused serious, irreparable damage; and in trying to save him, doctors were forced to breach the blood-brain barrier that prevents infection.

When Kear awakened, doctors were mystified. Science could not explain this. The doctors still thought his prognosis was poor: he would either die or spend the rest of his life as an invalid.

But then the impossible happened. Chase started talking. He started recognizing people. The doctors could barely believe what they saw. After less than a month in the hospital, Chase went home wearing a T-shirt that said "Miracle Man".

———

Miller, when he learned a few years ago that there was an annual Father Kapaun Day in the priest's hometown, drove halfway across the United States with his wife, Joyce. They reached Pilsen, a town so small he could walk the length of it in minutes, bad ankle and all.

In the decades since Kapaun shoved aside his executioner, Miller has worked, fished and raised two adopted children. He has lived a good life, he says.

In the big garden in back of his house, he raised watermelon, cantaloupe, collard greens, sweet corn, string beans, peppers, tomatoes, cucumbers and peas. Sometimes, looking at all those good things to eat, he remembered how he and the other POWs had nearly starved to death.

Lake Ontario lies only five miles away from Miller's house; he likes to go there, look out over the water. These moments, and all the other good things he enjoys, he owes to the man who saved his life.

He cries sometimes when he thinks of Kapaun. When he pulls off his sock at night, he looks at a lower leg forever reddish, black and blue; the ankle twisted, the skin pitted from grenade fragments. He would have never survived the death march if Kapaun had not carried him on his back.

Not knowing anyone in Pilsen, Miller asked around about Kapaun. Pilseners looked at him warily. So he told them that one day in North Korea he had lain in a ditch. And an enemy soldier had pointed the muzzle of a rifle at his head. "And then this guy came walking across the road."

At that point, people threw their arms around Miller's neck. There were still people in town who remembered Kapaun, baked kolaches and spoke Czech.

A local caretaker of the Kapaun legacy, Rose Mary Neuwirth, showed the Millers around. When Miller stepped onto the grounds of the Catholic church, he caught his breath. There was a bronze statue of Kapaun. He had his arm around a wounded soldier, who had a bandage wrapped around his injured leg.

———

Chase believes that Christ and Kapaun saved him. He knows that critics of Christianity and the Catholic Church will scoff at this. After news stories appeared about the Vatican's investigation of his cure as a Kapaun "miracle", cybercritics ridiculed his family, his faith.

"I don't care what they think", he said.

His neurosurgeon, Raymond Grundmeyer, told newspapers and the Vatican that Chase's survival is miraculous, and Chase believes him.

Other people believe Chase's healing was miraculous too. Women hug him. People shake his hand.

Chase says he's trying to figure out what he's supposed to do now. "I was given my life back", he says. "There must be a reason. What is it?" Not many things scare him, he says. That question does.

In church on Sundays, he says, he no longer mumbles his way through the Mass. He says his prayers for real.

———#———

As early as 1990, Dan Glickman, then a congressman from Kansas, asked the military to review whether Kapaun deserved the Medal of Honor.

Before the war ended, Kapaun was awarded the Distinguished Service Cross, the U.S. Army's second-highest honor for gallantry in combat. For this reason, and because so many years had passed, the military rejected Glickman's request.

Glickman's successor, Todd Tiahrt, took up the cause in 2001. He also got a no.

But Kapaun's friends would not give up; Dowe and the others kept writing letters, telling stories.

Learning that Kapaun's Distinguished Service Cross had been awarded for his battlefield courage, Tiahrt asked for a review of Kapaun's deeds in the prison camp. By coincidence, an instructor at West Point had begun researching a book about Korean War POWs. Lt. Col. William Latham, a veteran of the Persian Gulf War, interviewed Dowe, Funchess, Miller, Wood and many other men, and they all told him about Kapaun.

Latham collected a thick file of eyewitness accounts of Kapaun's heroism. He turned copies of it over to Kapaun's brother and sister-in-law, Eugene and Helen Kapaun.

They turned it over to Tiahrt, who gave it all to the army.

Those papers helped spur what happened next.

———#———

Enos and Bessie Kapaun with baby Emil

Emil Kapaun, age 6

Courtesy of Helen Kapaun

The Kapaun family home near Pilsen, Kansas

Emil Kapaun on the day of his First Communion, May 29, 1924

Emil Kapaun and his little brother, Eugene

Emil Kapaun home from seminary with his mother, Bessie

Emil Kapaun playing baseball at the family home in Pilsen.
Kapaun enjoyed sports of all sorts.

Emil Kapaun, age 18

Father Kapaun (center) with Marian and Louis Hurtig enjoying a summer day in Washington, DC, where Kapaun was attending Catholic University

Father Kapaun in Washington, DC, in 1947 when he attended Catholic University

Father Kapaun with children of his parish

Father Kapaun in front of the rectory in Pilsen

New assistant pastor of Pilsen, Father Emil Kapaun

From left, Fr. Flatley, Fr. Kapaun, and Fr. Way in Bhamo, Burma, during World War II. Father Kapaun would later reenlist and serve as a chaplain during the Korean War.

*Father Emil Kapaun repairing his bicycle, August 11, 1950.
Col. Skeehan notes on this photo that Fr. Kapuan carried apples
in his canteen cover.*

*Next page, bottom: Father Kapaun next to his pup tent somewhere
in Korea, August 1950*

*Father Emil Kapaun (right) and Capt. Jerome Dolan carrying an
exhausted GI off the battlefield in Korea, early in the war*

Father Kapaun conducting a field Mass on the hood of his jeep somewhere west of Taegu, Korea, on August 11, 1950

Next page, top:
Father Emil Kapaun celebrating Mass with chaplain's assistant Patrick J. Schuler, using the hood of a jeep as his altar, October 7, 1950. Kapaun was taken prisoner just a month later and died in a Chinese POW camp less than a year later.

Next page, bottom:
Father Kapaun preparing to conduct a field Mass on the hood of his jeep, August, 1950

Top photo: William Funchess as a young army officer

Lt. William Funchess, shown on the battlefield in Korea, was captured by the Chinese and met Father Emil Kapaun while they were prisoners of war.

Willian Funchess, second from right, while a prisoner of war in North Korea. This photo was taken months after Father Kapaun had died, and after Chinese guards began to feed prisoners better and supply warm clothing.

Above:
Mike Dowe's West Point
graduation photo.
After being captured, Mike
Dowe became one of Father
Kapaun's closest friends in
the POW camp.

Bob McGreevy's high school football photo. A year later he was in a North Korean POW camp and spent several months there with Father Kapaun.

Herb Miller of Pulaski, New York, was about to be executed by a Chinese soldier when Father Kapaun intervened and saved his life.

Herb and Joyce Miller's wedding photo

Chester Osborne was near death in the POW camp when Fr. Kapaun cradled him in his arms and gave him last rites, "just in case".

Bob Wood's military picture before leaving for Korea. He was captured and spent several months in a POW camp with Father Kapaun in the winter of 1950–1951.

Many honors came Father Kapaun's way after the war; Lt. Gen. Hobert Gay came to Wichita to present medals and other honors to Kapaun's parents, Bessie and Enos, standing alongside Bishop Mark Carroll of the Diocese of Wichita.

Next page, top: After the war and his release from a POW camp, Father Kapaun's close friend Ralph Nardella came to Wichita, bringing the crucifix carved by POWs in the camp to honor Kapaun. With him is Bishop Mark Carroll.

Next page, right (detail of the crucifix): Months after Father Kapaun had died, a Jewish Marine and POW, Jerry Fink, began hand-carving a 4-foot crucifix to honor the priest who was so beloved. It took months, and later cost Fink mistreatment at the hands of Communist guards, who later tried to confiscate the crucifix.
The cross is now on display at Kapaun Mount Carmel High School in Wichita, Kansas.

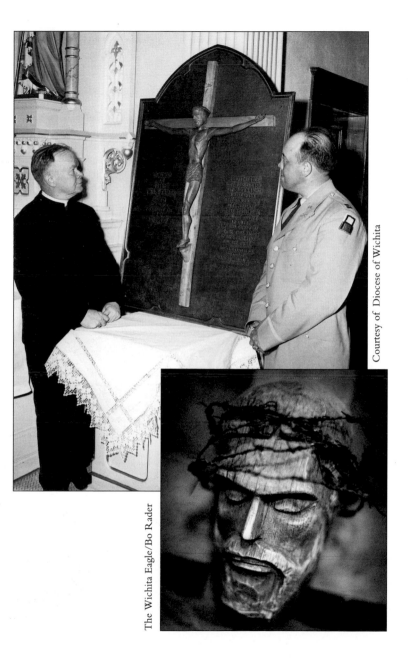

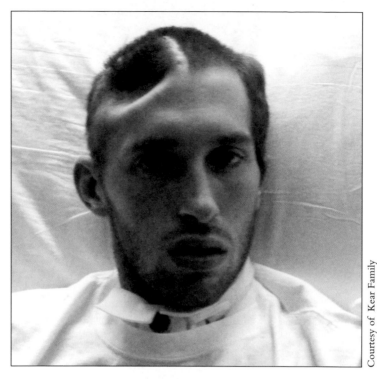

Chase Kear, with a hole in his head and his recovery in full swing, a few weeks after his pole-vaulting accident in October, 2008

Chase Kear and his parents, Paula and Paul, in the hallway of Wesley Rehabilitation Center in November 2008, just weeks after his near-fatal pole-vaulting accident

Chase Kear studying the statue of Korean War hero Father Emil Kapaun, who he believes intervened from heaven to help save his life

Chase Kear on a visit to St. John Nepomucene Church in Pilsen, carrying the processional cross Father Kapaun once carried when he was a priest there

The Wichita Eagle/Travis Heying

The Wichita Eagle/Travis Heying

Above: Nick Dellasega (center foreground, surrounded by friends and family) after a miraculous recovery attributed to the intercession of Father Kapaun

Facing page, top photo: Avery Gerleman, age 17, ready to start her senior year in high school, shows no signs of her eighty-seven day battle with death. Avery's recovery is being considered a miracle attributed to the intercession of Father Kapaun.

Facing page, bottom photo: Avery Gerleman's father, Shawn Gerleman, sitting in St. Patrick's Church, where he often prayed for his dying daughter, invoking the intercession of Father Kapaun

Bishop Michael O. Jackels, left, shakes hands with Vatican investigator Andrea Ambrosi after presenting him with a box containing more than 8,000 documents about Father Emil Kapaun. Ambrosi will read the documents and write a report to the Vatican regarding Father Kapaun's case for sainthood.

By summer 2009, a large number of Kapaun stories had been collected by Father Hotze, the judicial vicar of the Wichita Diocese now in charge of the sainthood investigation. The assignment had taken years. In order to declare that a particular person is in heaven with God, the Vatican first needs eyewitness accounts of the person's virtues. This step had been started before Hotze took on the case, and accordingly the Church had already named Father Kapaun a Servant of God in 1993. After the Vatican confirms everything Hotze has sent, it will declare Kapaun Venerable.

The next step, beatification, requires a miracle attributed to the person after his death, in other words, a miracle believed to be caused by his intercession in heaven. After the pope declares a person Blessed, another miracle needs to occur in order for the pope to give him the title of Saint.

Thus, to move Kapaun's case to the beatification stage, Hotze needed to provide a provable "alleged miracle", a cure that has no scientific explanation. He went in search of someone who had inexplicably recovered from an injury or illness after people had prayed to Kapaun.

Hotze found the Kears. Then he found a second family, the Gerlemans in Wichita, whose teenage daughter had overcome a catastrophic autoimmune disorder. At Hotze's request, Vatican investigator Andrea Ambrosi visited Wichita and interviewed both families and their doctors. He was surprised at what he learned.

In Ambrosi's experience in vetting sainthood cases, he had never heard such promising testimonials from witnesses; several doctors involved with both Wichita families were Protestants, and they were emphatic that these recoveries were real miracles. Ambrosi told Hotze that both alleged miracles looked good and that he would return.

Hotze had talked to many POWs by then. The stories he heard enriched not only the cause but his own life.

POW William Hansen, shortly before he died, described to Hotze how he and Kapaun used to sneak into places where Chinese doctors were treating dysentery or pneumonia. They would observe which medicines were being used and then return later to steal them for the American doctors.

Tibor Rubin, who won the Medal of Honor for his Korean War exploits, told Hotze how he had crouched terrified at the bottom of a foxhole one day, bullets flying. Kapaun jumped in beside him and casually reached inside his jacket.

"Hey," Kapaun said, "you want an apple? I got an apple."

Rubin said he won the Medal of Honor because his anti-Semitic sergeant tried to murder him by making him defend a hill alone against a mass charge by North Koreans. A survivor of Mauthausen death camp in World War II, Rubin was nevertheless a target of anti-Semitism in the army. Kapaun, he said, treated him with respect.

"He was nice to everybody", he said. "I was a Jewish person, but he always treated me like I was a Catholic person. It didn't matter to him who or what I was."

In one battle, Rubin was knocked out by an explosion and awakened to see Kapaun giving him the last rites.

"I was glad to see him", he said.

Rubin said he wrote a letter to "that Polish pope" years ago, recommending sainthood for Kapaun. Not knowing how long and complicated the canonization process is, he was puzzled over why the pope had not followed his advice.

In the Korean prison camps, Rubin had stolen food for the hungry. When he did so, he thought of his mother, who had taught him the Yiddish word "mitzvah", which means "good deed".

"When you give out mitzvahs, mitzvahs come back to you", his mother had said. "When you save somebody's life, you might save an entire nation, you never know."

Kapaun gave out a lot of mitzvahs, Rubin said. Doing good deeds was embedded deep in the fabric of his soul.

The priest's magnanimity had been noticed by a young woman from rural Kansas during peacetime, when no one suspected greatness.

After Kapaun had realized some people in his hometown did not easily accept him as their priest, he was transferred to another Czech-speaking parish in Timken. There he performed a marriage ceremony for World War II hero Marvin Finger and his bride, Helen Pechanec.

Helen had seen nothing unusual in the young priest before. But during the wedding, she said, there was a sudden flicker of power in Father Kapaun. It lasted only a moment, but she never forgot it.

"He said something to us as he married us," Helen said, "that he hoped that we'd live to see our children to the third or fourth generation. There was something about the way that he said it that just—well, it was somehow so powerful. . . . It just made me feel so good."

Helen also noted the trait Rubin had appreciated in Korea: Kapaun made a point of treating non-Catholics and non-religious people with the same warmth he showed to Catholics.

"Not all priests behaved that way", Helen said. "He never acted like he was being nice so he could get them in church. I had the impression that he made a special point of it because, the way he looked at it, all people are children of God and because you are a child of God, you are very important."

Kapaun's respect for everyone was evident when he visited the pool hall in Timken, Helen recalled. "Pool halls in little towns back then," she explained, "they were not big places for sin; they were where everybody went to have a beer and talk. But then, well, it was a pool hall.

"And there would be the town priest", Helen continued. He would be smoking his pipe, talking with folks and acting like he was no better than anybody else.

"When you think about it, Jesus did the same thing."

———#———

Hotze knows that proving the miracles attributed to Kapaun won't be easy. The Catholic Church wisely discounts most claims of divine intervention as impossible to verify.

Since 1858, thousands of sick and desperate people have sought miraculous cures every year at the shrine in Lourdes, France. Of the countless healings that have occurred after visits to the spring dug up by Saint Bernadette, only a few dozen have been deemed miracles.

While waiting for the Vatican's judgment on Kapaun's alleged miracles, Hotze has made helpful discoveries.

He and other priests were intrigued, for example, when they read Kapaun's sermons delivered in Pilsen while he was still a new priest. Some of these he had first written longhand in Czech. All of them were neatly typed in English.

The profound thinker that the priests encountered in these writings surprised them with the rhythmic cadences and poetic imagery of his sentences.

> The sorrows which we are to encounter on our journey thru life are covered with a veil.
> The forgiving of wrongs is the exercising of mercy.
> We must be on our guard that our temptations will not shake us like the wind does the reeds.

What surprised them most were passages in which Kapaun seemed to predict that he would be severely tested and to decide how he would act, how he would lead, in that situation: He would emulate Jesus, who led people by becoming their servant.

In his Palm Sunday sermon on April 6, 1941, Kapaun, only twenty-five years old, laid out the reasons for Christ's strategy in simple, vigorous sentences:

> Men find it easy to follow one who has endeared himself to them.
> A man finds it a pleasure to serve one who has saved his life.

The priest thought a great deal about leadership, as further evidenced in this paragraph:

> A great leader exerts a most powerful influence over the hearts and minds of his followers. Though the task of following such a leader is most arduous in itself, yet it becomes sweet and honorable, and comparatively easy in practice when the followers consider the dignity of the leader, the relation of the leader to his followers, the motives which prompt the leader, and the rewards which he offers.

Those thoughts, Hotze said, were the blueprint for Kapaun's sainthood. They explain why Kapaun steeled himself, nine years after he wrote them, to lead the same way Christ did, by laying down his life for his friends.

The men who endured the prison camps with Kapaun do not need further evidence to prove that he is a saint.

"We knew in the camp that he was a saint, while he was still alive", Funchess said. "It was obvious."

The Vatican's canonization process has baffled some of Kapaun's fellow prisoners. They saw him do heroic things that didn't seem to satisfy the Church's questions about him. Church officials asked whether Kapaun lived a life "above reproach". Soldiers grinned at this, recalling Kapaun's swearing.

When McClain, in a 2003 video interview with Archbishop Philip Hannan of New Orleans, said that he had watched Kapaun bring POW Chester Osborne back from the brink of death by cradling him in his arms and praying, Hannan asked whether his recovery was "immediate".

"No", McClain told him.

The Church seemed to be looking for uppercase, biblical-size miracles, like raising Lazarus from the dead.

The POWs never saw that happen in Pyoktong.

What they did see, Funchess said, were the sorts of lowercase miracles that all of us could do if only we had Kapaun's grit.

By that definition, Miller said, "That man's entire life was a miracle."

Was it not a miracle, he asked, when Kapaun shoved his executioner away?

"I was sure that guy was going to shoot both of us", Miller said. "We were in the middle of a battle. It was a miracle that he did not shoot us. Isn't that a miracle?"

The POWs say Kapaun saved innumerable lives—dozens on the battlefields, hundreds in the camps. By any standard, Funchess said, saving hundreds of lives in those conditions is incredible.

As far as Dowe is concerned, one of Kapaun's greatest miracles was giving hope to men who had none. "That kept a lot of us alive", he said. "When your life is so marginal, little things mean a lot."

The Church also asked Kapaun's fellow prisoners whether the priest won converts to Catholicism.

Yes, they said. Some men converted. But the broader answer is not so simple.

Osborne, according to his granddaughter Laurie Uhlman, came home from the war and told people he had survived imprisonment because of Kapaun. But he did not convert until 1974, more than twenty years after Kapaun had revived him.

Wood, who had helped carry Kapaun to the Death House, studied Catholicism when he got back home, but did not convert.

"I never found anyone in the Church who could match up to Father Kapaun", he said.

Funchess remained a Methodist; Miller, a Baptist.

McGreevy, born a Catholic, stopped going to Mass years ago after reading about sex scandals and cover-ups involving priests. Still devout, he could not bring himself to join any other faith. So in his home, he built a shrine. He acquired a small replica of the statue of Kapaun in Pilsen, set it beside his favorite chair and leaned Kapaun prayer cards against it. There he prays to Father Kapaun every day.

The questions from the Church, and the fifty-eight years it took for the Vatican to assign an investigator, puzzle POWs such as Miller.

Kapaun's whole life, they say, was an imitation of Christ:

Jesus risked his life to save others. Kapaun did that dozens of times.

Jesus said the last would be first. Kapaun gave away his own meager rations and exhorted officers to let enlisted men eat before they did.

Jesus washed the feet of his disciples. Kapaun washed the
sick and the dying.

"If I could talk to the pope," Miller said, "I'd tell him
that if he doesn't give sainthood to Father Kapaun, he might
as well close up the whole thing and never give it to anybody else ever again."

The survivors of North Korea's death camps do not
understand why canonization in the Catholic Church takes
so long, especially when the evidence of heroism is so overwhelming. It would probably be of little comfort to them
to learn that Joan of Arc, another saintly soldier and
prisoner of war, was not canonized until 1920, almost
five hundred years after her captors had burned her at the
stake.

Kapaun's friends don't understand all the whys and where-
fores of naming someone Saint in the Catholic Church. All
they understand is that they know of no other person more
deserving of that title.

In Korea, when Kapaun saved them, helped them and
encouraged them, they did not all believe in miracles. Some
of them did not even believe in God.

But they did believe in Father Kapaun.

⸺ # ⸺

When they heard the news in October 2009, former POWs
rejoiced.

The outgoing secretary of the army wrote Tiahrt that he
recommended Kapaun for the Medal of Honor. Admiral
Mike Mullen, then chairman of the Joint Chiefs of Staff,
concurred.

"I'm glad they are doing that for him", Dowe said when
he heard the news. "He sure did a lot for us."

The recommendation would go first to Congress, and then to Secretary of Defense Robert Gates.

Gates happens to be a graduate of Wichita's East High School, located five miles from Saint John's Chapel at Newman University, where Kapaun was ordained in 1940.

If Gates and Congress approved the recommendation, it would go to the president of the United Sates.

The POWs waited, expectantly, through the rest of 2009. They waited through all of 2010.

By February 2011, Dowe, disappointed with the delay, wrote yet another letter to a government official, asking once again that Kapaun be given the Medal of Honor.

Dowe was diplomatic. He knew how to express himself tactfully. But in this letter, written to staff members of Senator Pat Roberts of Kansas, Dowe let a little frustration show, even though he knew Roberts was an ally in pursuing Kapaun's cause.

Dowe was now in his mideighties, as were most of Kapaun's surviving POW friends. He and the others felt the same: What was taking so long? The joint chiefs had recommended the Medal of Honor; so had a secretary of the army. Still the recommendation had not moved.

In his letter to Roberts, Dowe volunteered to talk to anyone in power:

> While his immediate family now have, unfortunately, passed on, his recognition can yet serve as an inspiration to soldiers of the future as to the true meaning and value of the Code of Conduct of our Armed Forces as well as an example to the Chaplain Corps itself.
>
> I have known other CMH [Congressional Medal of Honor] winners personally and view Father Kapaun's heroics and accomplishments in POW Camp of being at least an equivalent level of valor, of having an enormous impact

on the enemy, and of having saved literally hundreds of lives at his own peril.

As I'm sure you are also aware, the road to the award of a CMH to Father Kapaun, as well as to his canonization by the Catholic Church, has been up and down to say the least.

We are reaching a period when those of us who were fortunate enough to know him and witness his heroics are fast disappearing from the scene.

———#———

With many saints, there is a transforming crisis.

Saul the Persecutor became Paul the Apostle when a blinding light struck him down on the road to Damascus. Augustine had a concubine. Francis of Assisi partied until dawn. All of these men experienced a dramatic moment of conversion.

But no one who knew Kapaun ever saw a road-to-Damascus moment. Hotze, after a decade of study, is sure Kapaun was born whole.

"Everybody I talked to said he was the same way as a boy", Hotze said. "In school when he finished his lessons he would look how to help other students complete their work. That was the same guy on the battlefield and in prison camps. He just felt compelled to help."

Kapaun reached his thirty-fourth year having done nothing remarkable. He grew up milking cows near a tiny, anonymous town. Fellow soldiers like Jerome Dolan, an Eighth Cavalry doctor, said he looked utterly ordinary except in battle.

The one recording of Kapaun's voice is a sermon delivered on Armed Forces Radio two months before he went to Korea. It reveals a voice of high pitch, with the inflections of a rural Kansas farmer, but with a Slavic flavor, with some consonants trilled or clipped the way some elderly Czech speakers in Pilsen still say them today. Kapaun's life until 1950 seems so quaint. The truth is that until the Eighth Cavalry Regiment landed on a beach in Korea in July 1950, Kapaun lived an exceptionally good life—so exceptionally good that on that very day, his reckless courage in battle began.

Joe Ramirez, who fought with the Eighth Cavalry all the way up the Korean peninsula, said he and many other soldiers saw Kapaun save wounded soldiers while running through gunfire from rifles, machine guns and submachine guns.

"Guys used to say, 'That man is crazy,' " Ramirez said.

American soldiers always tried to rescue their wounded, Ramirez said, but Kapaun would go farther out into enemy gunfire than anyone else dared.

Dolan later wrote about one such story, describing how Kapaun won the Bronze Star on July 26, 1950, only five days after the Eighth Cavalry had first gone into battle:

> One of my medics came to tell me that his platoon leader had been wounded in the leg and had ordered his men to leave him because he would burden them and cut their chances of getting out. I promptly told the colonel and he proceeded to command a reconnaissance-in-force, about two squads I believe, to go back and see if they could get out the wounded lieutenant.
>
> When I turned around, Father Kapaun and his assistant were gone with a litter. When the recon returned, Father Kapaun and the chaplain's assistant were with them, and they not only had brought out the platoon leader but another wounded man whose buddy had been killed so that no one realized he was missing at that time.

Whether Father Kapaun intended it or not, his courage in that action created a wonderful esprit de corps in that battalion. Despite several days in combat we had taken relatively light casualties and we had good officers, but it took the baptism of fire to show these green troops who had never seen combat before that they could survive this war if they took care of one another.

After Yong-dong-ni the rallying cry of that battalion was, "No matter what mess you get into, 1st Battalion will get you out!" And it was Father Kapaun who led the way while the rest of us were a little slower to react.

Kapaun was kind as well as brave. Dolan said that he and other GIs in a battle one day came upon a North Korean lying in a ditch, holding what looked like a grenade. The GIs wanted to shoot him, but Kapaun stepped forward and held out a canteen.

For a long time, the Korean stared at Kapaun as he gestured with the canteen. Finally, the Korean surrendered. Kapaun had been the one man who saw he was thirsty and hungry.

Raymond Skeehan, a captain in the Eighth Cavalry's medical unit, remembers Kapaun arguing with an officer in mid-battle. GIs were preparing to assault a hill full of North Koreans and their machine guns.

Kapaun pestered the commander: "Is this necessary? Isn't it kind of dangerous to attack this hill?"

The officer listened, postponed the attack—then watched the enemy retreat without a fight.

Skeehan, a part-time photographer, took the iconic photo of Kapaun in his vestments saying Mass on a battlefield, the blanket-covered hood of a jeep serving as an altar. Skeehan remembers the date: October 7, 1950. Kapaun was captured twenty-six days later.

The POWs remembered many great acts of gallantry like that, but also thousands of much smaller acts of kindness.

Before he was captured, when the Eighth Cavalry was moving north, an officer named Joseph O'Connor met Kapaun as the chaplain visited men from each regimental battalion, sometimes traveling miles from one battalion to the next. "He was a very laid-back, appealing man", O'Connor told Church investigators years later.

Kapaun told O'Connor that he wanted to get transportation to one of the companies. O'Connor said, "Well, sure, Father, we'll get you a jeep."

But Kapaun replied, "Now, I don't want to put you out."

Of this courteous reply, O'Connor said, "And that was the nature of the man."

Story after story describes how, before his capture, Kapaun not only performed hundreds of acts of generosity toward others but had built a constituency of enlisted men who loved him and would follow him.

Dolan wrote after the war:

> After we developed a reasonable defense line on the Nak-tong River in early August we actually had some dull, peaceful days. Then, either the American Legion or some beer company was sending beer and Coca-Cola over once a week.
>
> But then the beer suddenly stopped and the rumor was that [someone] pressured President Truman to protect these American soldiers from the demon rum.
>
> Morale fell, but here came Father Kapaun again, the kid from Kansas, and he came with his pockets bulging with apples. It wasn't the same as beer, but it was a welcome change from the dirty-mouth taste of C-rations mixed with too many cigarettes. And Father always carried two canteens of water so that you could wash things down if you had

not had a chance to fill your canteen.... Father found a way to build the morale.

The last time I saw Father Emil Kapaun was in late October 1950. We had been with one of the first units to cross the 38th Parallel and to capture the North Korean capital, Pyongyang. Our unit was then in reserve as the rest of the 8th Army moved up.

It was a quiet time, and Father and I each had rooms in what must have been a military academy. By modern standards it was not very elite but after the ground, it was marvelous.

I went by to see Father in his room and I found him writing letters to the families of the KIAs [killed in action] and the MIAs [missing in action]. I offered to help write some letters, but he said, "This is the chaplain's job."

He must have found some ink and paper and envelopes somewhere ... we had no source of paper, envelopes or ink. My own lovely Parker pen had run dry probably in mid-August.

But Father was the world's champion "scrounger." If you needed something, he would find it. And apparently he did the same thing in the prison camps, from what I heard later from fellows I talked to who had been in the prison camps.

He did allow me, however, to address the envelopes so I felt that the last time we were together I was of some help to him.

Skeehan also remembered Kapaun's kindness. "I saw him one day with a canvas bag of apples he'd found; he took them to an orphanage.

"None of us ever saw him nod off. We wondered when he slept."

Dolan recalled that Kapaun, before he was captured, had preached forgiveness when forgiveness seemed impossible.

"The *Pacific Stars and Stripes* had published a picture of men from the Fifth Cavalry Regiment who had been captured, tortured and executed", Dolan said. "After that atrocity, some of our troops were ready to retaliate in kind. I remember Father's sermon at the time—that as Christians and as Americans we would betray our heritage if we took revenge on the wounded or on prisoners."

On April 3, 2011, Chase Kear went pole-vaulting again at the Hutchinson Night Relays.

It was the second time he had done it since his recovery. No one could persuade him that this was a bad idea, not even Paula, his mother.

"Idiot!" he said with a laugh, a few days before the track meet. "That's what Mom calls me, an idiot. But I'm gonna rock it out, man!"

He laughed again.

He was now twenty-two years old. He felt invincible again.

Kapaun had given him back his life, he said. And he intended to live it. He pole-vaulted. And he failed to clear a single height. No matter, he said. It felt good to be in the air again.

On October 18, 2009, Chase and his family rode to Pilsen and visited the church where Kapaun had grown up, where he had served as an altar boy, where he had celebrated his first Mass.

The stone font where Kapaun was baptized stood near the altar. Morning light streamed through stained glass, shining through faces of angels.

After Mass, people talked, touched Chase's hand. They ate lunch in the church basement: roast beef, cake and Czech kolaches.

Edmund Steiner, ninety-three years old, one of Kapaun's boyhood chums, sat a few feet from the Kears. He said he and Emil went to schools run by nuns who whacked bad boys on outstretched palms with a wooden ruler. Not once did Kapaun get whacked, he said. The others got hit all the time.

"He never did anything wrong."

There was something oddly wonderful about Emil, he continued.

"All of us, we would swear and say bad words, but we never swore around him. It wasn't because he told us not to do it. It was because there was something about him. We couldn't swear around Emil."

Outside, as Steiner talked, Chase walked alone to the statue of Kapaun. The priest's left arm supported a soldier with a lower-leg wound.

Kapaun's right hand was outstretched.

———※———

The month before in Pulaski, New York, Miller, who still limps from his wound, told visitors that he had spent a lifetime since Unsan trying to know why Kapaun saved him.

Miller had not become a saint after all; he had become a calibration technician in a bearings factory in Syracuse.

"I get choked up sometimes thinking about it," he said. "Maybe God and Father Kapaun saved me for another reason."

After the war, he and Joyce adopted a girl and a boy. Those kids turned out real good, Miller said. He loves them; they love him.

"Maybe I was spared so that those two little kids could have a dad. Was that it? I don't know.

"I've thought about it every day since.

"Why me?"

———#———

At the Kapaun statue, Chase stood still, the morning sun rising over nearby treetops.

In the year since he came back to life, Chase has asked himself the same questions that have plagued Miller for fifty-nine years. Why is he alive? What is he meant to do now? He has no idea. It bothers him.

Do miracles happen? Chase believes they do. He believes in God. And like the old soldiers, he believes in Father Kapaun.

At the statue, Chase looked up at the bronze face staring down at him. The face has Kapaun's wide-set eyes, the cleft in his chin.

Chase looked into his face for a moment. Then he reached out and touched the hand of Father Kapaun.

9

TWO HEALINGS

When most people die, that's the end, or nearly so. But then there's that rare person who lives not only in memory or in books, but as something more: a living spiritual connection to something bigger than ourselves.

Father Emil Kapaun became one of those people almost from the moment he died in 1951. To this day, people all over the planet pray to him. When all seems lost, they call upon his name, as did these two Kansas families desperate to save the lives of their loved ones.

———

In October 2006, twelve-year-old Avery Gerleman scored a goal in a soccer game. She did not celebrate. She walked to the sidelines and threw up a gob of bright red blood onto the grass.

She told her coach, "I need to get back in there." The coach sat her down. After that, Avery's condition deteriorated.

Doctors in Wichita put Avery in a drug-induced coma and pushed a breathing tube down her throat. Avery's lungs filled with blood. Her kidneys shut down.

There was so much air and fluid leaking into her chest that her heart nearly stopped beating from the pressure. Doctors told Melissa and Shawn Gerleman that their daughter was going to die. Melissa cried. She and Shawn began to pray—to Jesus and to a priest from Kansas who had been dead for fifty-five years.

Doctors say what happened next is the most mysterious medical recovery they have ever seen.

Avery's two primary physicians are scientists, with intellectual allegiances rooted firmly in facts and sceptical reasoning. And they are Protestants, with none of the Gerleman family's background in the Catholic traditions of saints, guardian angels and miracles. But the doctors have told the Vatican that Avery's recovery is so unusual that there is no other explanation for what happened: They say it's a miracle.

Avery's parents say Father Emil Kapaun heard the prayers and tipped the scales in heaven.

Nick Dellasega wears a gadget in his chest. It gives a shock to his heart, if necessary. His heart recently seized up on him.

He doesn't look scared. He eats biscuits and gravy for breakfast, if it suits him. But he should have died on May 7, 2011, at age twenty-six.

A bunch of people saved him, keeping him tied to earth with the thin strands of a series of crazy coincidences. And prayer: A teenage cousin fell to his knees when Nick collapsed, and made a request to Father Kapaun.

Nick suspects that the prayer linked everything together and kept him alive. The coincidences are strange enough and the prayer notable enough that a Catholic Church investigator has reported Nick's story to the Vatican. The Church is evaluating whether Kapaun might have pulled a few strings in heaven.

Avery was playing soccer in a tournament in Fayetteville, Arkansas, when she spit up the blood. Melissa took her to a hospital there; she told Shawn on the phone that the doctors thought she had pneumonia. By that time, Avery was spitting up a lot more blood.

Melissa took her home to Wichita, and by then Avery was falling asleep or fainting from blood loss. Shawn took her to Wesley Medical Center; Avery passed out on the examining table.

For four days at Wesley, doctors thought Avery was merely dehydrated. But then a respiratory therapist, checking her over, became animated, calling in doctors and insisting that something was disastrously wrong with her lungs. Doctors realized the respiratory therapist was right.

Shawn at first was irritated: "Who the hell is this respiratory therapist who's turning our world upside down?"

Within minutes, he knew she probably saved Avery's life. Doctors began to work at a frantic pace, scanning Avery's lungs and other organs. What they saw made them work even faster. They put her on a breathing mask. They said it wasn't giving her enough oxygen, so they put her on a ventilator.

They saw blood in her urine and knew that her kidneys were also failing. They told Avery and her parents that they were ordering emergency procedures while having no clear idea of what was wrong with her.

In her hospital bed, no longer able to talk because of the breathing tube, Avery wrote a note to her father:

"What procedures?"

Shawn lied to her to keep her calm.

"They are procedures to make you feel better", he said.

After doctors ordered more procedures, Avery wrote down another question:

"Am I going to die?"

They told her no.

But by her bedside, as doctors put her into a drug-induced coma, her parents began to pray.

—⊣—

Nick's uncle, Dr. Mark Dellasega, is a veteran gastroenterologist, a stomach doctor who knows how to do CPR hand compressions on a dying man's chest. But as he says, it is something of a miracle that he was anywhere near Nick on the day in question.

It happened on May 7 in the Dellasega family's hometown, Pittsburg, Kansas. Dr. Dellasega lives in Greenville, North Carolina. By coincidence, he showed up the weekend of May 7 to visit family in Pittsburg.

But Dr. Dellasega has a serious addiction—to golf. He had no desire to watch the five-kilometer charity race Nick was running that Saturday morning. So at 7:00 A.M. the doctor went off with his brother, Doug Dellasega, to play thirty-six holes, telling family that he would catch up with them long after Nick's race.

"But the crazy thing is, we all played golf so badly", he said. "I got fed up after nine holes and went home.

"I decided to go watch the race after all. But I thought it was at the college [Pittsburg State University].

"So I jogged two miles down there. No one was there. I jogged back home.

"I finally figured out the race was to finish at Hutchinson Stadium [a field near downtown where Pittsburg high schools play football].

"I went down there. So the lucky thing was, I showed up just two minutes before Nick collapsed."

If he had been two minutes later, with all that jogging and dallying around, Nick likely would have died.

Dr. Dellasega's timely arrival was the first strand in a web that kept Nick alive. Nick's ego put the second strand in place. Toward the end of the 5K race, with his teenage cousin Caleb Dellasega racing to pass him, Nick kicked into a higher gear.

Nick had been a free safety for the Pittsburg State University football team, after all. He was only twenty-six, with a big chest, a skinny waist and a body in great condition. Getting outrun by a grinning eighteen-year-old cousin was not an option; Caleb would never let Nick forget.

"Nick turned around and told me he was going to beat me", Caleb said later. "He pulled ahead."

That was lucky. It meant Caleb was ten yards behind Nick when Nick collapsed. Had Caleb been ten yards in front, he would not have seen Nick go down. And he would not have shouted for help to Dr. Dellasega, who had just arrived at the finish line, only one hundred yards away.

In those first frantic days, and in the long days to come, Avery's two main doctors were Michelle Stuart Hilgenfeld, a young pediatric nephrologist in the first years of her career, and Lindall Smith, a pediatric intensivist who had worked in children's intensive care at Wesley for more than eleven years.

Hilgenfeld concentrated on the kidneys while Smith concentrated on the other organs. All were failing.

Shawn walked past a conference table and saw doctors paging through big, fat manuals, trying to match Avery's symptoms with any illness they could find. Smith later said that at times in those first few days there were as many as twenty doctors and other staff around that table, paging frantically through those manuals for clues.

Shawn saw that they didn't know what was killing his daughter.

The family prepared for a siege. Medical staff wheeled in two recliners alongside Avery's bed: one for Shawn, another for Melissa. They had so many machines hooked up to Avery that all the gear took up two bed spots.

They did not tell the Gerlemans this, but Smith and Hilgenfeld felt sick at heart.

Hilgenfeld, who recently had given birth to her fourth child, had to summon the strength to talk to the Gerlemans every day.

Smith had three boys, two of whom were Avery's age. Like Hilgenfeld, he wore a mask of professional detachment when he talked to parents. But though he had saved hundreds of children at Wesley, he sometimes lost children, too, and he sometimes cried after they died.

Smith said Avery's blood vessels were disintegrating everywhere; all her organs were failing.

"There's not a lot more we can do for her", he told the Gerlemans.

Melissa saw that Smith was pronouncing a death sentence. She glanced over at Shawn, who looked still and calm.

"She will live", Shawn said.

Avery had been a pretty girl, but she lay now unconscious and bloated. To force oxygen into what was left of her lungs, Smith was pumping so much air into her that her body and face puffed out.

Shawn was keeping a diary by then, and at Avery's bedside each night he wrote down names of doctors and nurses and medicines and machines. He also began to flip through a Catholic catechism, which contained a series of numbered paragraphs on Church teachings about intercessory prayers.

Like many Catholics, Shawn and Melissa believe in praying to saints as well as to God. Shawn began scribbling down paragraph numbers on the blank back page of a church bulletin he had found at the chapel of his church, Saint Patrick's.

The bulletin had been published by the Father Kapaun Guild, an organization dedicated to promoting Kapaun's cause for sainthood.

Shawn knew who Kapaun was: a Kansas farm kid turned U.S. Army chaplain and Korean War hero who had died while saving the lives of hundreds of prisoners of war.

Kapaun was still being investigated by the U.S. military and the Vatican—the military to determine whether to award Kapaun the Medal of Honor, the Vatican to determine whether to make him a saint. He was one of Shawn's heroes.

Shawn began scribbling down prayers to Kapaun.

"Father Kapaun," Shawn wrote on October 28, "take all the prayers said for Avery this week & lay them at the feet of the Lord. Intercede & obtain a miracle for Avery, full & immediate recovery for the Greater Glory of God."

Within days, hundreds of people in Wichita were praying along with Melissa and Shawn. E-mails the Gerlemans received showed that people all over Wichita and the United States began disregarding differences of belief and prayed Catholic prayers for Avery.

The charity race meant a lot to Nick. It was organized to memorialize Pittsburg native Dylan Meier, the former Kansas State University quarterback who had died in a hiking accident a year before. He had been Nick's friend, so Nick had driven in from Wichita—where he works at Koch Industries—and lined up to run with about two hundred others, including several cousins. He ran well enough to be in the top thirty as they neared Hutchinson Stadium and the finish line in the football field.

Caleb crept up on him. Nick told him he would beat him. He pulled away just as they ran onto the concrete pavement that divides Pittsburg Middle School from the bleachers on the north side of Hutchinson Field. A few feet more, and Nick would make a hard right turn off the pavement and run through a small gate onto the football field and toward the finish.

Had he paid attention, he would have seen Dr. Dellasega and a bunch of relatives at the finish line. The doctor could already see him. But Nick didn't see them. It was 10:37 A.M.

"All of a sudden Nick went down", Caleb said.

"I was ten yards behind. I stopped. Two guys ran to him. He went into convulsions; he was kicking his legs, moving his arms."

The men rolled Nick over. He had hit face first; he had two red skid marks, just above and just below his right eye.

"Nick's eyes were open, and it seemed like he had a smile on his face", Caleb said. "One of the guys poured water on Nick's neck from a bottle, and I thought Nick went down because he was hot."

Caleb stood over his cousin as other racers ran by. Thinking all would be well, Caleb ran for the finish line.

With fifty yards to go, he saw Dr. Dellasega at the finish line.

"Nick is down!" Caleb yelled.

The doctor did not hear.

Caleb yelled again. "Nick is down!" He pointed, back to the concrete drive.

Dr. Dellasega saw men kneeling around a body.

Dr. Dellasega was sixty-one years old. Two years before, when he had mild carditis, he came close to needing a heart transplant. But he was in good shape now.

He ran.

———*———

"All we did in those early days was put out one fire after another," Hilgenfeld said.

They kept Avery breathing with a breathing tube; Hilgenfeld kept her blood from going toxic, in the absence of functioning kidneys, by putting her on dialysis.

Both doctors kept bringing bad news.

Not long after Avery was sent to the pediatric intensive care unit at Wesley, Smith said he wanted to perform emergency surgery. The tissue sac around Avery's heart had filled with fluid, swelling so much that it was putting pressure on Avery's heart. They needed not only to drain the sac but to put a tube in there to drain fluid into her stomach. But Avery was now so fragile that Smith knew she would never survive a move to the operating room. He asked a surgeon to cut open her chest right in her room. The surgeon came to the room. He studied the girl and looked appalled.

"I don't know why we are even considering this", the surgeon said. "She's not going to make it, no matter what we do."

Melissa had followed the surgeon into the room as he came in; she heard what he said about her daughter. She was distraught. Hilgenfeld was irritated, and she saw that Smith was irritated, too, though he disguised it with his usual gentleness. Smith insisted the surgeon reconsider, implored him to look at the facts with a more open mind.

When the surgeon insisted, in front of her parents, that Avery was going to die, Smith dug in too, almost begging, with such passion that Hilgenfeld felt deeply moved. At last Smith pulled him aside, showed him x-rays and pleaded with him some more.

It was a lot to ask. The surgeon relented; he did the procedure.

"Father Kapaun, take the petition to the Lord", Shawn wrote in his diary. "Lord, forgive me for being selfish. I want a miracle healing.

"Heal her, Lord."

———//———

Dr. Dellasega fell to his knees and began pumping chest compressions directly over his nephew's heart. He had thought, when Caleb called out, that Nick had tripped or fainted. But he saw from the gray in Nick's face that this was cardiac arrest.

"Somebody call 911 right now!" he called out.

Somebody did, at 10:40 A.M., three minutes after Nick went down. Dr. Dellasega pumped his chest some more, felt for a pulse. No pulse. The doctor glanced around.

He knew that many communities in recent years have stashed small and surprisingly sophisticated heart defibrillators inside public and commercial buildings. If someone goes into cardiac arrest, any nonmedical person can lay the electrodes on and let the machine decide whether to shock the heart.

"Somebody needs to see if they can find us a defibrillator!" Dr. Dellasega called out. "Now!"

A few feet away stood a stranger that none of the Dellasegas had met. His name was Bryan Mahnken, and he works in the Pittsburg schools. What happened next might be coincidence. Or perhaps Kapaun really was looking out for Nick.

Whatever the reason, Mahnken, as he told the family, only a few days before had been handed a key to Pittsburg Middle School, a massive red brick building only steps away from Nick, who was staring sightlessly into the sky.

Mahnken had never set foot in the school. It was locked, the hallways dark. But there was probably a defibrillator in there. When he heard the doctor call for one, he ran to a door, inserted his key.

He had no idea where to look. Call it fate, call it what you will; Mahnken ran right to a defibrillator. He grabbed it.

"Avery," Shawn wrote to his daughter at her bedside, "I remember when you were two, we were at Scott City State Lake camping. There were foothills. You took the lead & said 'come on, guys, we can make it.' "

Shawn told Avery stories that she could not hear in her coma. Shawn told her how her mother was.

"I held your hand", he wrote in the diary.

He told her how her sister, Haley, a high school freshman, was doing. He told her that Haley loved her and Mom loved her and he loved her.

On November 4, 2006, at 4:20 A.M., Shawn wrote, "I ask Father Kapaun. I recognize his compassion for sick and injured & I ask him to present my petitions to [the] Lord [for] perfect healing of lungs & kidneys. I add—make this disease go away. Heal her, Lord."

Smith and Hilgenfeld were struck by how calm the Gerlemans looked. Many parents, faced with the impending death of a child, will yell at doctors and nurses, curse them in despair. But every time Hilgenfeld talked to them, Avery's parents were cordial. They asked perceptive questions.

They were not as calm as they appeared. At night, when doctors or nurses arrived in Avery's room, Shawn would wait until they left, then pull a blanket over his head and sob under the fabric.

⟶———⟶

It kept going that way for Nick, luck so crazy good that it seemed miraculous. Mahnken ran out of the school and right into a woman who happened to be a physician's assistant. Mahnken didn't know how to work a defibrillator; she did. She grabbed it. She ran to Nick and the doctor and pulled the leaves with the electrodes out of the machine.

Dr. Dellasega by that time had yanked Nick's shirt up to his armpits, baring his chest. Nick still had no pulse. The doctor and others doing CPR had kept Nick's blood going. But this could give him only the slimmest of chances. The physician's assistant stuck the electrode leaves onto Nick's chest at 10:42 A.M., only five minutes after Nick went down.

Zap.

Nothing. No pulse, no respiration. The doctor thought his nephew was dead, or close to dead. Two minutes passed. An ambulance arrived. Two muscular, bearded guys got out.

They moved fast. Micah Ehling and Jordan Garner had answered hundreds of emergency calls, far more than a hundred involving heart seizures. They knew what a lethal cardiac arrest looked like. They thought this one looked lethal the moment they saw Nick's face.

This call hit them both in the guts. They recognized their boyhood friend Nick Dellasega immediately. They loaded him in the ambulance, with Ehling doing chest compressions. At 10:45 A.M., eight minutes since Nick collapsed, they shut the ambulance doors. Ehling, huddled inside, kept doing chest compressions, sure that Nick was a dead man.

"I know what a face looks like when the soul leaves the body," he said, "and that's what Nick looked like."

But then Ehling, frantically trying to save his friend, searched for a pulse again.

———#———

Hilgenfeld found what she believed to be the name of Avery's disease: pulmonary renal syndrome. It is an autoimmune disorder in which the body's defense system goes haywire, and antibodies that defend against germs, viruses and toxins suddenly turn on the body in what Hilgenfeld called a deranged metabolic state. Avery's antibodies were attacking membranes and blood vessels everywhere, including in the lungs and kidneys. She was self-destructing.

Hilgenfeld ordered what to the Gerlemans sounded like a desperate procedure: therapeutic plasma exchange. A machine takes blood from the patient and spins it down in a centrifuge, separating the solid blood cells and platelets from the plasma. The plasma is then discarded, along with any of the haywire antibodies, and the blood is put back into the patient, along with new plasma or replacement fluid. The treatment took two to four hours; over the course of Avery's eighty-seven days in the hospital, she received ten such treatments, along with kidney dialysis twenty-four hours a day.

Shawn walked into her room one day and counted thirty-two machines hooked up to Avery. She had tubes in her chest, her sides, her groin. She had the tube in her throat, and IVs in both hands, both arms and one foot.

Shawn and Melissa did what they could to keep their daughter clean, to "let her keep her dignity", as Shawn said later. They washed phlegm from her face, her neck, her chest. They picked and brushed dead skin from her hands and face.

Their home in northwest Wichita was virtually empty, neglected. Melissa felt as if they had abandoned Avery's older sister, Haley, a freshman at Bishop Carroll High School. But Haley was outwardly as confident and upbeat as her parents: Haley told Melissa that she would take care of herself, that Avery would survive, that no one should give up.

Outside the ambulance doors, with extended family weeping around him, Dr. Dellasega felt sick for the first time that day. He had felt calm and poised in the ten minutes that he and others pushed on Nick's chest; adrenaline and training had kicked in.

But he knew he would now have to call his brother, Nick's father, Joe Dellasega, and tell him the news. Nick's parents were out of town this weekend. The Dellasega cousins and in-laws wept. He wanted to weep himself.

He looked at the ambulance, which sat there, not moving. As a doctor, he had spent a lot of time around EMTs, and he got a little frustrated now. EMTs have their way of doing things; instead of racing to the hospital, for example, they sometimes like to spend time at the scene, "stabilizing the patient".

"Forget that here", Dr. Dellasega thought. "We're three minutes from the hospital."

Dr. Dellasega walked to ambulance doors and opened them. He saw something that puzzled him. The EMTs looked surprised. Almost happy. Ehling gave the doctor a quick look; the doctor got the idea he wasn't wanted here.

"What's going on?" the doctor said.

With a flick of his hand, Ehling told the doctor to shut the doors. But just before the doors shut, Ehling spoke.

"We've got a pulse."

Just before they arrived at the emergency room, Nick startled the EMTs again. As Ehling prepared to stick a breathing tube down Nick's throat, Nick opened his eyes. Ehling felt a surprise deeper than any he had ever felt on a call. He had never seen this in a cardiac-arrest case. Neither had Garner. Nick should be dead, or brain-damaged.

Nick blinked. Then looked surprised. Then embarrassed when he saw that his chest was bare. Then he saw the face of his childhood friend, about to shove a plastic tube down his throat.

"Micah!" Nick said. "What's going on?"

———#———

Avery's thirteenth birthday on October 31, about two weeks into the hospital siege, passed in a blur of the usual crises: She had a high fever; her heart rate was too high; she had staph and yeast infections.

Hilgenfeld was doing another plasma procedure. Alarm bells on the machines hooked to Avery's body went off again and again.

Even if the plasma-cleansing treatment stopped the disease from eating through more of the girl's kidney and lung membranes, Hilgenfeld thought, the damage already done to those organs was probably catastrophic. Hilgenfeld and Smith both thought death would be only a matter of time.

If Avery did not die, she would need constant dialysis, eventually a kidney transplant. Kidneys, if they shut down for a day or two, sometimes don't start working again, and Avery's kidneys had been shut down for weeks.

Yes, Hilgenfeld thought, Avery would either die or live for a while in a persistent vegetative state, her brain gone. Smith had saved many children, but he had also said goodbye to a few who were ruined like that.

The doctors did not confide these thoughts to the parents, but both doctors said enough for them to know that the case was nearly hopeless. Avery was slipping ever downward, her tough little soccer-athlete body fighting a last stand.

"We will do what we can for her, but this is mostly between God and Avery", Hilgenfeld had told the parents early on. She still felt that way.

Sometimes things happened that shocked the doctors. Two weeks after he put Avery on a breathing tube, Smith reduced the amount of sedative that was keeping her in a coma and pulled out the tube. To his amazement, she breathed on her own, opened her eyes, recognized her parents and tried to mouth words to them.

Smith felt tears in his eyes; he had thought she would be nearly brain-dead by now, so this seemed miraculous. Had he known it wasn't the last such surprise, he might have felt more hope, but he didn't. So many other things kept going wrong.

Shawn sobbed under his bedside blanket in Avery's room again on the night of November 8. Sometimes Melissa and Shawn would lift Avery up so the nurses could change the sheets; they lifted her easily. Eventually she lost so much weight that Shawn could hold her in the air without bracing his elbows on his torso, as though she were no more than a cornstalk. She had entered the hospital weighing ninety-eight pounds. At her weakest, she weighed sixty-six.

Her parents massaged and moved her legs, which were growing stiff from lack of use. They fluffed her pillows, arranged her feet and legs so she would be more comfortable.

At 1:45 on the morning of November 9, Shawn, feeling desperate, prayed a prayer over Avery and left the hospital.

He drove north from Wesley to Saint Patrick's; he went into the small adoration chapel near the church.

The chapel was open all hours, with its small altar and exposed Communion host, which the Catholic faithful believe brings them the presence of Christ.

Shawn knelt and prayed. Then he lay facedown on the floor before the altar, resting his head on his hands. He did not so much pray as beg.

"Heal my daughter", he said. "Free her of this disease. Hear me, O Lord. May I have a fraction of faith; may it be enough to heal my daughter."

As Avery's condition continued to deteriorate, and the autoimmune disorder continued to ravage her internal organs, her doctors began seeing more surprises.

They still thought she was going to die. But about a week or two after Smith had pulled out the ventilator tube, Hilgenfeld discovered that Avery's kidneys were functioning. This baffled Hilgenfeld. With the kidney damage she had seen in early biopsy reports, this should not be happening.

Five weeks after Avery's kidneys had shut down, they came back online; and Hilgenfeld knew of no other case like this in the medical literature. She and Smith had done all they could, and with modern medicine they could do a lot. But the restored kidney function defied explanation.

Hilgenfeld is a Mennonite. Her denomination does not share the Catholic belief in saints working miracles from heaven. But she knew, because she had seen some unexplainable things before, that patients sometimes recover in ways that surpass human understanding.

———

The rest of the earthbound story about Nick Dellasega's survival can be told in only a few words.

Doctors determined that Nick did not have clogged arteries or heart disease. They determined he had an electrical rhythm problem.

They sent him home after a few days with an implanted pacemaker, which not only monitors his heart but shocks it back into proper rhythm if necessary.

But let us go back to that scene on the pavement. Nick is down. Soon he is surrounded by Dr. Dellasega, Bryan Mahnken, the physician's assistant, his cousin Caleb and all the others who performed so ably that day, or who wept by his side.

Only a few of them, Dr. Dellasega included, noticed one other person off to the side.

He was small in stature and played no physical role in Nick's survival. But Nick and the doctor and everyone else who was there that day now think he might have played the crucial role. He was kneeling on the concrete, praying.

His name is Jonah Dellasega. He is Nick's cousin and Caleb's younger brother. And though he was only fourteen, he possessed poise and purposefulness that he had cultivated through a short lifetime of devotion to God.

Jonah was running in the five-kilometer race too, wearing a bright red T-shirt with the logo of the Pittsburg State University Gorillas printed on the front. He came running up to Nick's prone body just after Dr. Dellasega started CPR. The Dellasega women also came running up now and, distraught at Jonah seeing Nick like this, shooed him off to the side.

But no matter. Jonah walked a few feet from the group. He dropped to his knees and began to pray, to Jesus and Mother Mary and Father Emil Kapaun.

On November 1, All Saints' Day in the Catholic Church calendar, Father Eric Weldon—a priest at Saint Patrick's, the Gerlemans' church—asked everyone in the parish to pray for Avery's life and recovery.

Shortly afterward, when she saw birthday balloons beside her bed and realized she had missed her birthday, Avery became upset, and they consoled her. Then later, she woke up again with no memory of these things. She saw the balloons, and they made her happy.

Meanwhile, though, there were few encouraging signs: Her body continued to leak blood and water where the tubes stuck out of her; she got smaller and lighter, and the alarm bells and buzzers on her machines kept sounding— each alarm perhaps foretelling Avery's imminent death.

But while this was going on, encouraging things also happened. On Thanksgiving Day, November 23, after Hilgenfeld had gotten over the shock of seeing the girl's kidneys performing well, she said to Avery's parents, "If someone does not know God, introduce them to Avery Gerleman."

Slowly but surely, as November drifted toward December, medical victories became more frequent. Doctors pulled tubes out of Avery's thin body one by one. They began to reduce the medications. Avery began to eat bits of soup and other foods.

On November 25, Avery, a huge University of Kansas basketball fan, watched part of the Jayhawks' game against the Florida Gators, though she fell asleep halfway through.

The next day, as it dawned on her how her parents had sat by her side day and night, she told her dad how much she liked how he and her mom took care of her. Avery told them how grateful she was.

Jonah Dellasega prayed to Kapaun while Nick was taken to the hospital and kept it up after he went in there.

He knew the whole story about the priest and U.S. Army chaplain: the battlefield heroism in the Korean War, the way he had saved hundreds of prisoners in the camps after his capture. He knew that Kapaun had given away his food while starving, inspired men to love and help each other even as hundreds died. He had blessed the guards as they abandoned him to die.

Nearly everyone in the Dellasega clan is a devout Catholic. When Dr. Dellasega came down with mild carditis two years before, the whole extended family got together and prayed to Jesus and Mary and Father Kapaun to save him. But Jonah, a thoughtful, skinny kid, was by no means devout merely because of family. He had thought deeply about his faith for years on his own.

Two years before, already committed to following Jesus, he had learned about Kapaun and decided to model the rest of his life after the priest.

So when the family shooed him away, Jonah prayed to Kapaun, as he had prayed to him many times already.

Sceptics might look at this story and point out that the time sequence is off. They could rightly say that Jonah did not start praying until after the doctor began CPR, long after that series of coincidences that led the golf-addicted doctor to abandon his round and then to jog in the right direction.

How could a prayer save a life in advance of the prayer? There is an answer to this question. And the Church investigators know about it, and they decided to forward this story to the Vatican.

If Kapaun really is a soul in heaven, and if he really has the ability to receive messages from us mortals on earth, then Jonah has been filling up Kapaun's in-box for years now, asking the saint for guidance, for strength and to watch over all of Jonah's loved ones.

On December 4, the hospital staff put Avery through physical therapy that caused her almost torturous pain; she stood up, a sight that no doctor had dared to hope for.

By that time, because of the e-mails the Gerlemans were getting, they knew that all over the world people, individually and in prayer chains, were praying for her—people in Italy, England and other places far and wide.

People in many churches in Wichita were praying to Jesus, as well as to Kapaun and other saints. Avery's Wichita Attack soccer team, including the Protestant players, were saying Rosaries for her with their Catholic teammates. Other parents in Wesley Medical Center's pediatric intensive care unit, struggling to keep their own children alive, were praying for Avery.

Every day she became more awake and aware, and Smith and Hilgenfeld and other doctors kept finding surprises. Later, after they had scanned her lungs and kidneys, they saw what seemed impossible: no scarring, not much tissue damage. It was like peering into a building after a fire and seeing no burn marks on the walls.

The healthy tissue did not make sense. Avery's lungs had been so damaged that Smith had told Avery's parents that if their daughter survived, she would have to be on oxygen for the rest of her life.

But six months after Avery walked out of Wesley, she was playing competitive soccer again.

Was it a miracle?

"I don't know, but I think so", Avery said. "I think it was, but I struggle with what I think about.

"It seems weird: Why would God choose me?"

Her parents told her that perhaps her story was meant to reveal God's glory to those who doubt or disbelieve.

But after thinking about her survival for a long time, Avery, at seventeen and with one year to go in high school, told her parents that she wanted to turn the meaning of her survival into something more tangible. She said she would become a doctor or a nurse and spend the rest of her life helping the sick.

Three years after Avery's recovery, in 2009, Vatican representative Andrea Ambrosi came to Wichita to investigate Kapaun's alleged miracles.

Ambrosi came to interview the Gerlemans and the family of Chase Kear, the track athlete who had inexplicably survived a pole-vaulting accident in October 2008. The recovery of Dellasega occurred in 2011, two years after Ambrosi's visit.

The Church's effort to sort out Kapaun's candidacy for sainthood, dormant for decades, had heated up after Hotze had reported the cases of Chase and Avery to the Vatican.

Ambrosi, a layman and a lawyer by training, had not come to validate the cases, but to play devil's advocate, to see whether he could poke holes in the stories. But as he told Hotze later, he was surprised at what he found.

Chase had smashed his skull on the ground when he missed the vaulting mat in practice. His neurosurgeon told Ambrosi that Chase's survival was a miracle. Chase's parents and family had prayed hundreds of prayers to Kapaun in the weeks during which Chase hovered near death.

In their meeting with Ambrosi, Shawn and Melissa did nothing to gild or embellish the story of how their daughter survived. Shawn had struggled with the decision about whether even to talk to the Vatican representative. He knew that Jesus and Kapaun had stressed, by word and action, that humility was a virtue to be cultivated every day.

He believed the same. He did not think that he or his family should be thought of as special or as better than anyone else. He did not want his teenage daughter to become distracted, or even vain, by being put on some sort of miracle pedestal created either by the media or the Vatican.

He and Melissa also felt compassion and empathy for the other parents they had met in the hospital's intensive care unit who fought—and sometimes lost—grievous battles to save their own children.

Shawn and Melissa also believed that because of God's grace, Kapaun and many other good people already were saints in heaven, whether the Gerlemans talked to the Vatican or not. They and Avery were sure about several things, though: that God is good, that God and the saints listen to prayer, but that God's true purposes in matters of life and death are mysteries beyond our reckoning.

Shawn and Melissa told the story matter-of-factly to Ambrosi. They did not say Avery's recovery had happened "immediately", or even quickly, even when prompted by Ambrosi's questions. They did this despite knowing that saying so would boost Kapaun's chances.

They also gave credit to Avery's doctors, Hilgenfeld and Smith, and to the many others who gave wonderful medical care to their daughter.

Those two doctors, though, took a different tack. They told Ambrosi that they were stunned by Avery's survival, by her lack of tissue damage, by her apparently complete recovery. They told Ambrosi, through his Italian interpreter, that there was no scientific explanation for what happened. They were so passionate about this that at one point, Hotze saw that both Hilgenfeld and Smith had tears in their eyes as they talked to Ambrosi.

Later, when Hotze drove Ambrosi to Wichita's Mid-Continent Airport, Ambrosi told him, through his interpreter, that both the Kear and Gerleman cases were unusually good, especially the Gerleman case. He told Hotze that in all his years of poking holes in miracle stories for the Vatican, he had never heard a story as persuasive as the one told by Avery's doctors.

The case for Kapaun was looking hopeful indeed, Ambrosi said. And he added that it was a good thing that Hotze had found such good Catholic doctors to tell Avery's story to the Vatican.

"But, Dr. Ambrosi," Hotze said, "they are not Catholic."

Ambrosi, startled, gave Hotze a long look. Then he spoke again, and the interpreter relayed his words:

"You're kidding me!"

"No, I'm not", Hotze said.

Even the Protestants thought Avery's healing was a miracle.

EPILOGUE

In March 2012, Bishop Michael Jackels, from Kapaun's home diocese in Wichita, visited Rome, undertaking a pilgrimage to the Vatican that most bishops make every five years. While there he prayed and touched base with old friends (Jackels used to work at the Vatican and knows Pope Benedict XVI).

He also did some old-fashioned lobbying on behalf of Father Kapaun. He met with Angelo Amato, prefect of the Congregation for the Causes of Saints, the group now studying all the documents Father Hotze had gathered about the priest, soldier and Korean War hero.

Jackels told what he knew about the man, and Amato listened. Then Amato remarked that the investigation of Kapaun's case would be expedited.

It could still take years, though.

"The Vatican thinks in terms of centuries", Jackels explained.

In April 2011, nearly sixty years after Kapaun died, his friend, the nuclear physicist Mike Dowe, went to Washington, D.C., again to make the case for Kapaun's Medal of Honor.

He visited Rep. Mike Pompeo from Wichita, who had lobbied for the medal for months and who was keenly aware that time is running out for Kapaun's POW friends, who have long hoped to see their hero's Medal of Honor ceremony.

Pompeo, awestruck at meeting Dowe, gathered his whole staff and called his wife in so she could meet him too.

"It was great for us to meet this man, a friend of Father Kapaun who is, in his own right, an amazing American, doing super-important things for our country", Pompeo said.

But Pompeo had to tell the old soldier that there was more delay in store.

It had taken months for Congress to pass legislation enabling the military to authorize the medal after all that time.

Then several more months had passed since the secretary of the army and the chairman of the Joint Chiefs of Staff had recommended the award for Kapaun. Pompeo assured Dowe he would stick with the task.

Months after Dowe's visit, in the spring of 2012, Pompeo learned that Secretary of Defense Leon Panetta had signed a written endorsement of the medal for Kapaun. The paperwork went to the White House, where it awaits the approval of President Barack Obama, who was busy overseeing two wars, a struggling economy and a reelection campaign.

Pompeo called the White House, asked for a meeting with White House staff and told them the story of Kapaun.

"They were kind", Pompeo said. "They listened, indicated they would make sure the information I gave them got to where it needs to be."

Dowe and all Kapaun's other old friends are still waiting.

Publisher's note:
At the time this book went to the printer, the Medal of Honor had not yet been awarded to Father Kapaun; however, it had been unofficially announced that the chaplain would soon be given this honor.

ACKNOWLEDGMENTS

Deputy editor/print Tom Shine was the primary editor for the Kapaun newspaper series and book. Sherry Chisenhall, editor and senior vice president of the *Wichita Eagle*, helped supervise the Kapaun series and book and helped edit the story text. John Boogert and Lori O'Toole Buselt produced the *Miracle of Father Kapaun* online at www.Kansas.com/kapaun. Cori Dodds and Michael Roehrman copyedited the series. Bo Rader helped Travis Heying extensively, taking still photos and gathering archival and historical photos for the series, the book and Travis' DVD *The Miracle of Father Kapaun*. Kevin McGrath contributed editing help. Lt. Col. William Latham, Ret., a historian and an instructor at the U.S. Army's Command and General Staff College at Fort Leavenworth, consulted with us to make sure the series was accurate from a military-history perspective. Kapaun's friend and fellow prisoner of war Mike Dowe read the book manuscript and made many crucial changes, additions and suggestions. Special thanks to Jean Hays, Brian Corn, Marcia Werts and Stan Finger of the *Eagle*'s staff; Helen Kapaun; Rev. John Hotze, judicial vicar of the Catholic Diocese of Wichita; Stacey Jenkins of KPTS-TV; U.S. Rep. Mike Pompeo, R-Kansas, and Rose Mary Neuwirth of Pilsen, Kansas.

APPENDIXES

PRINCIPAL CHARACTERS

Dr. Clarence Anderson was the Unsan hero soldiers admired equally with Kapaun for rescuing wounded men under fire. He also behaved heroically in the prison camp, saving lives. He and Esensten worked to save Kapaun as the priest's health declined in spring 1951.

Nick Dellasega collapsed while running a road race in Pittsburg, Kansas. He recovered after a remarkable sequence of chance events and prayers to Father Kapaun. Wichita Diocese officials have shared his story with the Vatican.

Lt. Mike Dowe stole food to try to keep Father Kapaun alive and became one of his closest friends in the POW camp. He co-wrote the *Saturday Evening Post* story in 1954 that made Kapaun a national hero. He has lobbied, testified and written about Kapaun's heroism for sixty years. Now in his mideighties, he works full time as a nuclear physicist.

Dr. Sidney Esensten was captured several weeks after Kapaun. With other camp doctors, he tried to save lives as hundreds of POWs died. When Kapaun got dysentery, Esensten conspired to create a fake dysentery epidemic; when the guards gave the prisoners medicine, Esensten gave it to Kapaun. A Jew, Esensten often debated religion with Kapaun and deeply admired him.

Maj. Jerry Fink had little interest in Christianity until he heard about Kapaun, who died before Fink's capture. Fink, a fighter pilot, an artist and a Jew, spent months carving a crucifix to honor Kapaun. Guards tried to confiscate it after the war; the POWs threatened to stay behind with it if they did.

Lt. William Funchess took an ailing Kapaun into his camp hut and slept beside the priest to warm him. He nearly came to blows when guards came to take Kapaun away to die. After the war he worked for the extension service in South Carolina, developing cutting-edge farming techniques. He lives in Clemson and still attends Clemson University football games.

Avery Gerleman, who doctors were certain would die, resumed playing soccer six months after leaving the hospital. She and her parents were interviewed by a Vatican investigator. She is thinking about becoming a nurse.

Rev. John Hotze has traveled the country for more than a decade helping the Vatican consider Kapaun's fitness for sainthood. He is a priest and the judicial vicar for Kapaun's home diocese in Wichita. His first church as a priest was Kapaun's former parish in Pilsen, Kansas.

Chase Kear smashed his skull when he missed the mat during pole-vault practice at Hutchinson Community College in 2008. Family and friends prayed hundreds of prayers to Kapaun. Kear's neurosurgeon told Vatican investigators that Kear's survival cannot be explained by science.

Lt. Walt Mayo briefly saved Kapaun from capture at Unsan by ordering a rifle volley that killed Kapaun's captors. In camp, Kapaun amused himself by telling Mayo in Latin: "Ne illegitimi carborundum esse." Mayo, a World War II vet who survived four months in a German prison camp, would repeat in English: "Don't let the bastards get you down."

Lt. William "Moose" McClain slept beside Kapaun for months to keep them both warm; they made a game out of picking lice off each other. McClain, a combat officer in World War II and Korea, wrote a vivid, unpublished memoir about both wars.

Cpl. Robert McGreevy was a star high school football player from Cumberland, Maryland. Only nineteen when captured, he nearly starved to death but rallied every time Kapaun sneaked into the enlisted men's quarters to talk. He nearly died in the Death House in 1951, but recovered while praying to the soul of Kapaun. He still lives in Cumberland; he has prayed to Kapaun every night since the war.

Sgt. Herb Miller played dead in a ditch at Unsan after a grenade shattered his ankle. He was about to be executed when Kapaun shoved the enemy soldier aside and carried Miller away; Kapaun supported Miller for miles on the march to the POW camp. Miller, who also saw action in World War II, still limps. He lives in Pulaski, New York, five miles from Lake Ontario. He sometimes goes fishing there.

Lt. Ralph Nardella fought at Unsan, then repeatedly risked his life in prison by defying guards, saying Rosaries and nearly starting a fight with guards taking Kapaun away to die. Nardella proposed to create a shrine to Kapaun; the result was the four-foot crucifix now at Kapaun Mount Carmel High School in Wichita, a school Nardella and other POWs helped found with their own money.

Cpl. Joe Ramirez was baptized by Kapaun on the beach moments after the Eighth Cavalry entered the war with an amphibious landing in 1950. At Unsan, Ramirez was wounded five times, but carried other wounded to the prison camp. Ramirez lives in Houston; his son is a retired U.S.

Army brigadier general; one grandson serves in the military police, and another is a captain with the Twenty-Fifth Infantry Division.

Lt. Bob Wood volunteered for Unsan though he had been shot a few weeks before. When guards ordered Kapaun to the Death House, Wood and three others formed an honor guard to carry him. Wood wept when Kapaun blessed the guards as they entered the Death House. He lives in O'Fallon, Missouri; his camp eating spoon hangs on the living room wall, but his Silver Star is hidden in a drawer.

TIMELINE OF FATHER KAPAUN

April 20, 1916—Born Emil Joseph Kapaun in Pilsen, Kansas

June 9, 1940—Ordained a priest at what is now Newman University in Wichita

June 20, 1940—Celebrates his first Mass at Saint John Nepomucene in Pilsen, Kansas

1943—Appointed auxiliary chaplain at the army air base in Herington, Kansas

November 1943—Named pastor of Saint John Nepomucene parish

August 1944—Enters the U.S. Army Chaplain Corps

March 1945–May 1946—Serves in India and Burma

January 3, 1946—Earns promotion to captain

July 1946—Leaves the chaplain service

October 1946—Does graduate work at Catholic University in Washington, D.C.

1948—Rejoins the army's chaplain service

December 1949—Makes final visit home to Pilsen

July 1950—Ordered to Korea from Japan, a month after North Korea invades South Korea

August 2, 1950—Earns Bronze Star for heroism in action

November 1950—Captured near Unsan, North Korea

May 23, 1951—Dies in a prison camp in Pyoktong, North Korea

August 18, 1951—Posthumously awarded the Distinguished Service Cross for his actions at Unsan

1993—Named Servant of God by the Roman Catholic Church, the first step toward possible canonization

October 1, 2009—Recommended for the Medal of Honor

Timeline of Korean War

1950

June 25—War breaks out when North Korea invades South Korea

June 30—U.S. troops enter war

July 8—Gen. Douglas MacArthur named UN commander in Korea

Mid-July—Father Kapaun and the Eighth Cavalry Regiment ordered to Korea from Japan

September 15—MacArthur's forces land at Inchon and begin the liberation of South Korea

October 1—MacArthur drives North Koreans out of South Korea; American troops pursue North Korean army across the thirty-eighth parallel north, the dividing line between the two Koreas

October 24—American forces approach the Yalu River on the Chinese border

November 1—People's Republic of China enters the war on the side of North Korea

November 2—Father Kapaun taken captive at the Battle of Unsan

November 25—UN forces forced to retreat from Yalu River under Chinese onslaught

1951

April 11—President Truman relieves MacArthur of his command

May 23—Father Kapaun dies in a POW camp in North Korea

June 21—UN troops push the Communist forces out of South Korea

July 10—Truce talks start

November 27—Cease-fire line established at thirty-eighth parallel north

1953

July 27—War ends with signing of armistice at Panmunjom calling for a demilitarized zone and voluntary repatriation of prisoners. The thirty-eighth parallel north is established as a boundary between North and South Korea.

SOURCES

Books and Periodicals

Dowe, Raymond Michael, Jr. "The Ordeal of Chaplain Kapaun". *Saturday Evening Post*, January 16, 1954.

Maher, William L. *A Shepherd in Combat Boots: Chaplain Emil Kapaun of the 1st Cavalry Division*. Shippensburg, PA: White Mane, 1997.

Tidings (Archdiocese of Los Angeles). "Long Beach Physician Tells of Heroic PW Padre". October 16, 1953.

Other Sources

Material for this book also was obtained from Helen Kapaun; the archives of the Catholic Diocese of Wichita; the archives of the *Wichita Eagle* and Beacon Publishing; St. John Nepomucene Church in Pilsen, Kansas; the Father Kapaun Guild (www.frkapaun.org); Kapaun Mount Carmel High School in Wichita, Kansas; Shawn, Melissa and Avery Gerleman; Chase and Paula Kear; Dr. Joe Davison; Rev. John Hotze; Raymond Skeehan, a former captain of the U.S. Army Eighth Cavalry Regiment; Marian Hurtig; former POWs Mike Dowe, William Funchess, Herbert Miller (and wife, Joyce), Bob McGreevy and Bob Wood; Laurie Uhlman, granddaughter of former POW Chester Osborne; U.S. Rep. Todd Tiahrt; U.S. Rep. Mike Pompeo; Sam Sackett, communications director for Todd Tiahrt; historian Lt. Col. William Latham, Ret.; Rose Mary Neuwirth of Pilsen; Pam Nardella, the daughter of former POW Ralph Nardella.

INDEX